In Good Company

Hospitality from the Homes and Hills of Virginia

The Junior League of Lynchburg

This book is dedicated to the people of the Lynchburg area.

When you're among friends, you're always In Good Company.

"Rose Garden" photograph by Max Eckert courtesy of *Veranda*
"Monument Terrace" photograph courtesy of the City of Lynchburg

Cover and all other photography by Robert DeVaul

Copyright © 1999 Junior League of Lynchburg, Inc.
2102 Rivermont Avenue
Lynchburg, Virginia 24503
(804) 846-6641

Library of Congress Number: 99-071711
ISBN: 0-9614766-1-3

Edited, Designed and Manufactured by
Favorite Recipes® Press
An imprint of

FRP℠

P. O. Box 305142, Nashville, Tennessee 37230
(800) 358-0560

Manufactured in the United States of America
First Printing: 1999   12,500 copies

Cover photo inset—*Berkeley*
Cover photo background—*Wolf Branch Farm*
Title page photograph—Dining room of Mr. and Mrs. Lamar Cecil

This cookbook is a collection of favorite recipes, which are not necessarily originals.

Contents

Introduction

The Junior Welfare League, a 1926 service organization, was accepted into the Association of Junior Leagues of America in 1929, thus becoming the Junior League of Lynchburg. From the very beginning, members of the Junior League have been involved in projects relating to issues affecting women, children, historic preservation, education, and the environment.

The Junior League of Lynchburg is an organization of women committed to promoting voluntarism and to improving the community through the effective action and leadership of trained volunteers.

A primary goal of the League is to identify community needs and implement projects to address those needs. To provide financial support for community-based projects such as Families and Schools Together, Children's Theatre, and the Community Health Project, the League participates in ongoing fundraisers such as Bargain Mart.

Many past projects of the Junior League of Lynchburg now function as independent entities. The Adult Day Care Center; Kids' Haven: A Center for Grieving Children; and Amazement Square, a children's museum, all began as League projects but now have independent 501(c)(3) status and separate boards of directors.

For more than 70 years, the women of the Junior League of Lynchburg have been a caring, committed group of volunteers. Many are professionals; others are full-time wives and mothers. All are special in that they take time from busy lives to help meet the needs of others in our community as well as benefit from the volunteer and leadership training the Junior League provides. The Junior League of Lynchburg takes pride in its work and its volunteers who make so many good things possible for Lynchburg and the surrounding areas.

First Impressions

Cheese Pennies

$^1/_2$ cup (1 stick) butter, softened
1 cup shredded Cracker Barrel Cheddar cheese
1 cup flour
$^1/_2$ (1-ounce) package onion soup mix
1 teaspoon salt
$^1/_4$ teaspoon baking powder

Combine the butter and cheese in a medium bowl and mix well. Add the flour, soup mix, salt and baking powder. Mix until well blended.

Shape the dough into 1-inch-diameter logs. Cut into $^1/_4$-inch-thick slices. Place cut side down on ungreased nonstick baking sheets. Do not allow sides to touch.

Bake at 375 degrees for 10 minutes. Cool on the baking sheet for 1 minute. Remove to a wire rack to cool completely.

May tightly wrap the cheese logs in plastic wrap and refrigerate until ready to bake.

Store the baked cheese wafers in a covered tin for up to 2 months.

Serves 10 to 12

Sustainer Cheese Straws

10 ounces extra-sharp Cheddar cheese, shredded
1 cup (2 sticks) butter, softened
$2^1/_2$ cups sifted flour
1 teaspoon salt
1 teaspoon (or more) cayenne

Place the cheese in a mixer bowl and beat for 2 minutes. Add the butter and beat for 10 minutes or until light and fluffy. Add the flour, salt and cayenne and mix well.

Place the cheese mixture in a cookie press. Press into 5-inch strips onto nonstick baking sheets. If you have no cookie press, you may place the cheese dough in a sealable plastic bag, cut off a small corner from the bottom of the bag and squeeze the dough onto the baking sheets.

Bake at 350 degrees for 10 minutes or until the edges are light brown. Cool on the baking sheets for 1 minute. Remove to wire racks to cool completely.

Serves 10 to 12

Photograph on overleaf:
Point of Honor
by Robert DeVaul

Herb Focaccia

1	(11-ounce) can refrigerated French bread dough	1	teaspoon freshly ground pepper
2	tablespoons olive oil	1	teaspoon basil
1	teaspoon oregano	1/2	teaspoon thyme
1	teaspoon (or less) kosher salt		Marinara sauce (optional)

Unroll the dough and place in a 10x15-inch baking pan. Press to flatten slightly. Press the handle of a wooden spoon into the dough to make indentations at 1-inch intervals. Drizzle the olive oil over the dough. Sprinkle with the oregano, salt, pepper, basil and thyme.

Bake at 375 degrees for 10 minutes or until lightly browned. Do not overbake.

Cut the bread into rectangles. Serve warm with the marinara sauce.

Serves 8

Mini Ham and Swiss Sandwiches

1/4	cup (1/2 stick) butter, melted	1	(20-count) package Pepperidge Farm party dinner rolls
1	tablespoon poppy seeds		
1	tablespoon finely chopped onion	8	ounces sliced deli ham
2	teaspoons prepared mustard Dash of Worcestershire sauce	4	ounces Swiss cheese, sliced

Combine the butter, poppy seeds, onion, mustard and Worcestershire sauce in a bowl and mix well.

Remove the bread from the package in 1 large piece. Do not separate the bread into rolls. Slice the bread horizontally into halves, being careful to keep both the top and bottom halves of the bread in complete pieces. Brush the cut sides of the bread with the butter mixture.

Layer the ham and cheese on the bottom half of the bread. Cover with the top half. Place the sandwich in the original foil pan.

Bake at 325 degrees for 20 minutes. Cut into individual sandwiches and serve warm. Use a pizza cutter for easy cutting.

Serves 10

Point of Honor
overlooks the city of Lynchburg and the James River. The origin of the property's name is not documented, but since "Point of Honor" is a term associated with duels, it may have been a favored spot for settling conflicts. Built around 1815, the home features a unique semi-octagonal double-bay façade, featured on only a handful of the nation's houses from this time period. Originally home to Dr. George Cabell, Sr., the two-story Federal mansion was a showpiece in nineteenth-century Lynchburg and continues as a central attraction in the city's history. Cabell administered his most famous patient's last medical treatment when he gave Patrick Henry what turned out to be a lethal dose of mercury in an attempt to save his life.

Green Onion Chiffonade in Pastry Shells

1/4	cup (1/2 stick) butter		Pepper to taste
4	to 6 green onions, thinly sliced	6	tablespoons grated Parmesan or Reggiano-Parmigiano cheese
1/4	cup sour cream		
1/2	teaspoon celery seeds	24	miniature pastry shells

Melt the butter in a medium skillet over medium heat. Add the green onions. Cook for 10 minutes or until tender, stirring occasionally.

Stir in the sour cream, celery seeds and pepper. Simmer for 2 minutes, stirring occasionally.

Remove the skillet from the heat. Stir in the Parmesan cheese.

Arrange the pastry shells on a baking sheet. Spoon the filling into the pastry shells.

Bake the filled shells according to the package directions.

May prepare the filling without the Parmesan cheese up to 1 day in advance. Reheat the filling in a skillet over medium heat, stirring occasionally. Remove the skillet from the heat and stir in the Parmesan cheese. Spoon the filling into the shells. Bake according to the package directions.

Serves 12

Havarti Cheese Bake

1	(8-count) can crescent rolls	4	to 8 ounces Havarti cheese, sliced

Unroll the crescent rolls. Divide the dough into 2 rectangles and press the perforations to seal.

Place 1 of the dough rectangles on an ungreased baking sheet. Top with the cheese slices. Cover with the remaining dough. Pinch the outer edges of the dough together to seal.

Bake at 350 degrees for 15 minutes or until golden brown.

Cut into portions using a pizza cutter. Serve with fresh fruit.

Serves 4 to 6

Shrimply Delicious

3	ounces cream cheese, softened	1	tablespoon fresh lemon juice
1	cup sour cream	2	tablespoons finely chopped green bell pepper
1	envelope Italian salad dressing mix	1	cup cooked peeled shrimp

Combine the cream cheese and sour cream in a medium bowl and mix until blended.

Stir in the salad dressing mix, lemon juice and green pepper. Add the shrimp and mix lightly. Refrigerate for 1 hour or until chilled. Serve with favorite crackers.

Serves 6

Tequila Marinated Shrimp

1/4	cup olive oil	1/4	cup tequila
3	tablespoons finely chopped onion	1/4	cup fresh lime juice
5	garlic cloves, minced	2	tablespoons chopped cilantro
2	pounds fresh peeled shrimp with tails	1/8	teaspoon salt

Heat the oil in a large skillet over medium heat. Add the onion and garlic. Cook for 3 minutes or until tender, stirring occasionally.

Add the shrimp and tequila. Bring to a boil, stirring occasionally. Simmer, uncovered, for 3 to 5 minutes or until the shrimp turn pink, stirring occasionally.

Place the shrimp mixture in a medium bowl. Add the lime juice, cilantro and salt and mix lightly.

Refrigerate, covered, for 8 to 10 hours, stirring occasionally. Drain and serve.

Serves 10 to 12

Fruit Kabobs with Mint Dip

1 **pound seedless green grapes**
1¼ **pounds small fresh strawberries**

Cantaloupe or honeydew melon cubes
Mint Dip

Thread the grapes, strawberries and melon cubes alternately onto 6-inch bamboo skewers.

Garnish with sprigs of fresh mint. Serve with the Mint Dip.

Serves 10

Mint Dip

32 **ounces plain low-fat yogurt**
¾ **cup mint jelly**

½ **cup finely chopped fresh mint**

Combine the yogurt and jelly in a bowl and mix until blended.

Refrigerate, covered, until serving time.

Whisk the dip and stir in the fresh mint just before serving.

Lean Bean Dip

2 **(15-ounce) cans black beans, drained, rinsed**
1 **(16-ounce) can refried beans**
1 **(16-ounce) jar salsa**
½ **medium onion, finely chopped**
⅛ **teaspoon pepper**

1 **(8-ounce) can whole-kernel corn, drained, or kernels of 1 ear fresh white corn, cooked**
1 **or 2 fresh tomatoes, chopped, or 1 (16-ounce) can chopped tomatoes, drained**

Combine the black and refried beans, salsa, onion and pepper in a medium bowl and mix well. Stir in the corn and tomato. Let stand for 30 minutes before serving.

Serves 10 to 12

Hot Broccoli Dip

1 (5-ounce) jar cheese spread	1/2 cup finely chopped celery
1 (10-ounce) can cream of mushroom soup	1 (4-ounce) can sliced mushrooms, drained
1/4 teaspoon garlic powder	1 (2-ounce) package sliced almonds
1 (10-ounce) package frozen chopped broccoli, thawed	1 tablespoon minced onion
1 (8-ounce) can water chestnuts, drained and chopped	1/4 to 1/2 cup (1/2 to 1 stick) margarine, cut up

Combine the cheese spread, soup and garlic powder in a large microwave-safe bowl. Mix until well blended.

Add the broccoli, water chestnuts, celery, mushrooms, almonds and onion and mix well. Stir in the margarine.

Microwave on High for 6 minutes or until the margarine is melted and the mixture is heated through, stirring occasionally.

Keep the broccoli dip warm in a slow cooker on Low or in a heated chafing dish.

Serve with corn chips, crackers or French bread cubes. The broccoli mixture is also delicious over baked potatoes.

Serves 16

In 1841, Samuel Henry McGhee, a Scottish immigrant to the area, acquired land near the Blue Ridge Mountains not far from Thomas Jefferson's Poplar Forest. The McGhee residence was based on a Jeffersonian model and built in the late 1840s, using bricks that were made on the property. Some of these same bricks were used to build nearby St. Stephen's Episcopal Church. McGhee named the property **Berkeley** after the colonial governor whom he admired. A builder, McGhee constructed many of the area's brick houses and farmed tobacco on the property's acreage. Nearly 100 years after the completion of the original structure, Andrew Gleason, who owned the property, added flanking wings, columns, electricity, and plumbing.

Bargaín Mart Salsa

1   (16-ounce) can white Shoe Peg corn, drained
1   (16-ounce) can kidney beans, drained
1   (16-ounce) can black beans, drained
5   large tomatoes, chopped
1/2 (4-ounce) can chopped jalapeños or green chiles
1   yellow banana pepper, chopped
1   red bell pepper, chopped
1/2 medium green bell pepper, chopped
1   medium red onion, chopped
3   green onions, sliced
1   cup red wine vinegar
1   cup extra-virgin olive oil
    Juice of 4 limes
2   tablespoons sugar
1   tablespoon chopped fresh parsley or cilantro
1   tablespoon chopped fresh oregano
    Salt and pepper to taste
    Flour tortillas

Combine the corn, beans, tomatoes, jalapeños, peppers, red onion and green onions in a large bowl and mix lightly.

Whisk the vinegar, olive oil, lime juice, sugar, parsley, oregano, salt and pepper in a bowl until well blended. Add to the bean mixture and mix lightly.

Refrigerate, covered, for 2 hours or longer to allow the flavors to blend.

Cut the tortillas into wedges. Place on a baking sheet sprayed with nonstick cooking spray.

Bake at 350 degrees for 10 to 15 minutes or until lightly browned. Serve with the salsa.

May substitute purchased tortilla chips or corn chips for the homemade tortilla chips.

Serves 20

Salsa with Papaya

1	pound tomatoes, seeded, chopped	1/2	cup chopped fresh basil
1/2	English cucumber, peeled, chopped	1	shallot, minced
1/2	ripe medium papaya, chopped	2	tablespoons fresh lemon juice
2	green onions, chopped	2	tablespoons olive oil
		1	teaspoon sugar
			Salt and pepper to taste

Combine the tomatoes, cucumber, papaya, green onions, basil and shallot in a large bowl and mix lightly.

Whisk the lemon juice, olive oil, sugar, salt and pepper in a small bowl until well blended. Add to the tomato mixture and mix lightly.

Refrigerate, covered, for 4 hours or longer.

Serve with tortilla chips or over hot cooked chicken or fish.

Serves 6 to 8

Hot Office Party Dip

16	ounces cream cheese, softened	5	banana peppers, chopped
8	ounces shrimp, cooked, peeled, coarsely chopped	4	cherry peppers, chopped
		1	medium tomato, chopped
1	medium onion, chopped	3	garlic cloves, minced

Combine the cream cheese, shrimp, onion, peppers, tomato and garlic in a slow cooker.

Cook, covered, on High for 2 hours, stirring occasionally. Serve with crackers.

May substitute precooked peeled frozen shrimp for the fresh shrimp. The dip may be made ahead, covered and refrigerated. Heat as directed before serving.

Serves 20

*Like Rome, Lynchburg is called the **City of Seven Hills**. Lynchburg's seven peaks represent original or annexed areas of the city's beginnings. Daniel's Hill is named for Judge William Daniel, Jr., who owned and divided the 800-acre Point of Honor property. Also named for a resident is Garland Hill, which was named after Sam Garland, Jr., a prominent lawyer in the city's early days. Diamond Hill and White Rock Hill both bear names reflective of their surrounding geographical features. College Hill is so-named because of the area's pre-civil war military school, which functioned as a hospital during the war. Federal Hill surrounds the site of the now defunct Federal Hotel. Franklin Hill is said to be named after Benjamin Franklin.*

Corolla Crab Spread

8 ounces cream cheese, softened	1/4 teaspoon hot pepper sauce
1 cup Miracle Whip or mayonnaise	6 ounces lump crab meat
1/4 teaspoon Worcestershire sauce	3 green onions, chopped Slivered almonds

Combine the cream cheese, Miracle Whip, Worcestershire sauce and hot pepper sauce in a bowl and mix until well blended.

Stir in the crab meat and green onions. Spoon into a shallow glass baking dish. Sprinkle with the almonds.

Bake at 350 degrees for 15 to 20 minutes or until hot and bubbly. Serve with crackers.

Serves 10

Hot Onion Soufflé

12 to 16 ounces frozen chopped onions (3 to 4 cups), thawed	24 ounces cream cheese, softened
1 (10-ounce) package frozen spinach, thawed	2 cups grated Parmesan cheese
1 (16-ounce) can artichoke hearts, drained, chopped	1/2 cup mayonnaise

Drain the onions and spinach and squeeze to remove the excess moisture. Combine the onions, spinach and artichokes in a medium bowl.

Mix the cream cheese, Parmesan cheese and mayonnaise in a bowl until well blended.

Add to the spinach mixture and mix well. Spoon into a shallow 2-quart soufflé dish.

Bake at 425 degrees for 15 minutes or until golden brown.

Serve with corn chips, assorted crackers or cocktail pumpernickel bread slices.

Serves 6 to 8

Shrimp Mousse

11	ounces cream cheese, softened	1	pound cooked, peeled, deveined shrimp
3	tablespoons mayonnaise	1	onion, chopped
1 1/2	tablespoons fresh lemon juice	1	green bell pepper, chopped
1	or 2 envelopes unflavored gelatin	1/2	cup chopped celery
		2	hard-cooked eggs, chopped
3	to 4 tablespoons cold water	1	teaspoon hot pepper sauce
			Salt and pepper to taste

Mix the cream cheese, mayonnaise and lemon juice in a large bowl.

Soften the gelatin in the cold water in a small saucepan. Heat until dissolved, stirring constantly. Cool completely, add to the cream cheese mixture and mix well. Add the shrimp, onion, green pepper, celery, eggs, hot pepper sauce, salt and pepper and mix well.

Pour into a fish-shaped mold. Refrigerate until firm. Unmold onto a large plate. Add a stuffed green olive slice for the fish "eye" if desired. Serve with melba toast rounds.

Serves 20 to 25

Tomato Cheese Spread

8	ounces cream cheese, softened	8	ounces Cheddar cheese, shredded
1/2	cup (1 stick) margarine, softened	1	cup chopped peeled tomatoes
1	teaspoon salt	1	small onion, chopped
1/2	teaspoon cayenne	2	cups chopped pecans or walnuts
	Garlic powder to taste		

Combine the cream cheese, margarine, salt, cayenne and garlic powder in a food processor container and process until smooth.

Add the Cheddar cheese, tomatoes and onion and mix well. Shape into a log or ball. Roll in the pecans to coat evenly. Serve with crackers.

May stir the pecans into the mixture before shaping and serve in a bowl as a cheese spread. Prepare the day ahead for best flavor. The cheese ball may be frozen, tightly wrapped, for up to 2 months.

Serves 12

Elegant Artichoke Soup

½	cup (1 stick) butter		1	cup sliced canned artichoke hearts
1	cup chopped carrot			
½	cup chopped green onions		2	egg yolks
1	rib celery, chopped		1	cup whipping cream or half-and-half
1	bay leaf			
	Pinch of thyme			Salt and pepper to taste
4	cups chicken broth or consommé			

Melt the butter in a large skillet over medium-high heat. Add the carrot, green onions, celery, bay leaf and thyme. Cook until the vegetables are tender, stirring occasionally.

Stir in the broth. Bring to a boil. Reduce the heat to low. Simmer for 15 minutes, stirring occasionally.

Add the artichokes. Simmer for 10 minutes, stirring occasionally. Cool slightly and discard the bay leaf.

Whisk the egg yolks in a bowl with the whipping cream until well blended. Season with the salt and pepper. Stir into the slightly cooled soup. Cook the soup over medium-low heat until heated through, stirring frequently; do not boil. May serve immediately or refrigerate, covered, and serve chilled.

May omit the eggs and substitute skim or low-fat milk for the whipping cream to make a reduced-fat, reduced-cholesterol version of this tasty soup.

Serves 6

Bean and Hominy Soup

3	(16-ounce) cans Great Northern beans	1	(11-ounce) can whole-kernel yellow corn, drained
1	(16-ounce) can hominy	2	cups water
1	(14-ounce) can no-salt-added stewed tomatoes	2	bay leaves
		1	tablespoon dried cilantro
1	(10-ounce) can diced tomatoes with green chiles	1	teaspoon ground cumin
		1	cup shredded reduced-fat Cheddar cheese
1	(11-ounce) can bean with bacon soup		

Combine the undrained beans, undrained hominy, stewed tomatoes and tomatoes with green chiles in a Dutch oven. Add the soup, corn and water and mix well.

Stir in the bay leaves, cilantro and cumin.

Bring to a boil over medium-high heat, stirring occasionally. Reduce the heat to medium-low. Simmer, covered, for 30 minutes.

Remove and discard the bay leaves. Ladle the soup into warm soup bowls.

Sprinkle each serving with some of the Cheddar cheese.

Serves 12

Riverviews, *an artist's colony located along Lynchburg's riverfront, provides studio and residential space for area artists. The former Craddock-Terry shoe warehouse, built in 1898, offers space and light as well as spectacular views of the James River. In addition to designating this building as an important facility to area artists, Riverviews also marks the resurgence of interest in Lynchburg's downtown and riverfront area.*

Bloody Mary Chili

1	pound ground beef	2	teaspoons chili powder or to taste
1	onion, chopped	1/2	teaspoon ground cumin or to taste
1	green bell pepper, chopped		Salt and pepper to taste
2	garlic cloves, minced	2	tablespoons cornmeal (optional)
1	jalapeño, seeded, minced		
1	quart Bloody Mary mix		
1	(16-ounce) can kidney beans		

Cook the ground beef in a large saucepan until brown and crumbly, stirring frequently; drain well.

Add the onion, green pepper, garlic and jalapeño. Cook until the onion and green pepper are tender, stirring occasionally.

Stir in the Bloody Mary mix and undrained beans. Season with the chili powder, cumin, salt and pepper.

Stir in the cornmeal gradually to make the chili a slightly thicker consistency.

Simmer, covered, until heated through or until serving time.

Adjust the seasonings before serving.

May pour the chili into a slow cooker to cook for several hours or keep hot for later serving.

Serves 4 to 6

Cream of Carrot Soup

2	pounds carrots, peeled, shredded	1/4	teaspoon freshly ground pepper
3	(14-ounce) cans chicken broth	1/4	cup (1/2 stick) butter
1/2	cup fresh dill, chopped	1	medium onion, chopped
2	tablespoons sugar	1/4	cup flour
1/2	teaspoon salt	1	cup whipping cream
		1	cup milk

Place the carrots, broth, dill, sugar, salt and pepper in a large stockpot. Bring to a boil over medium-high heat. Reduce the heat to low. Simmer for 20 minutes or until the carrots are tender.

Melt the butter in a large skillet over medium-high heat. Add the onion. Cook for 4 to 5 minutes or until the onion begins to turn brown, stirring frequently.

Stir in the flour. Cook for 3 minutes, stirring constantly. Add to the carrot mixture in the stockpot and stir until well mixed. Remove the stockpot from the heat. Let stand until cool.

Pour the soup in small batches into a blender or food processor container. Process until smooth. Return to the stockpot.

Stir in the whipping cream and milk. Cook over medium heat until heated through, stirring occasionally.

Serve warm or chilled. Garnish with sprigs of fresh dill and sautéed carrot curls.

Serves 8 to 10

Confederate General Jubal Early prevented the destruction of Lynchburg and its vital railroads in 1864. A portion of the earthwork created as the Outer Defense Line, which contributed to the retreat of General David Hunter, is preserved at **Fort Early**. A nearby obelisk pays tribute to the senior officer in Lynchburg's Civil War battle. A native of Franklin County and a West Point graduate, Early adopted Lynchburg as his home following the war. He is buried in the city's Spring Hill Cemetery near the site of his 1864 headquarters.

Friendly Chicken Soup

1	(2- to 3-pound) chicken, cut up	1	teaspoon salt (optional)
2	quarts water	1	chicken bouillon cube (optional)
1½	cups chopped carrots	½	teaspoon poultry seasoning
1	cup chopped celery	½	teaspoon pepper
½	cup chopped onion	½	teaspoon dried sage
½	cup barley	1	bay leaf

Combine the chicken and water in a large soup pot. Simmer, covered, until the chicken is tender.

Remove the chicken pieces. Discard the skin and bones and cut the chicken into bite-size pieces. Let the broth stand until cool and skim off the fat.

Return the chicken to the soup pot. Add the carrots, celery, onion, barley, salt, bouillon cube, poultry seasoning, pepper, sage and bay leaf.

Simmer, covered, for 1 hour or until the vegetables and barley are tender. Remove and discard the bay leaf.

This soup is perfect for a cold night. Just add salad and crusty bread. It is also nice to take to a sick friend.

Serves 6

Curried Lima Bean Soup

1	(10-ounce) package frozen lima beans	1	teaspoon chopped parsley
2	tablespoons butter	½	teaspoon dried tarragon
¼	cup sliced onion	½	cup half-and-half
1	teaspoon curry powder	1¼	(10-ounce) cans chicken broth

Cook the lima beans according to the package directions until tender, adding the butter, onion and curry powder.

Pour the mixture into a blender container. Add the parsley, tarragon and half-and-half. Process until smooth. Add enough of the broth gradually to make of the desired consistency, processing constantly.

Pour the soup into a saucepan and heat to serving temperature to serve hot. May serve at room temperature or chilled.

Serves 4

Chilled Cucumber Soup

1/2	cup beef consommé	2	tablespoons fresh lemon juice	
3	tablespoons sour cream	1	cup whipping cream	
1	large cucumber, peeled, chopped		Salt and white pepper to taste	
2	small pickling cucumbers, peeled, chopped	1	tablespoon chopped fresh dill	
3	tablespoons chopped onion			

Place the consommé, sour cream, cucumbers, onion and lemon juice in a blender or food processor container. Process until smooth.

Pour into a medium bowl. Stir in the whipping cream, salt and pepper. Refrigerate, covered, until chilled.

Pour into soup bowls. Sprinkle each serving with some of the dill. Garnish with thin slices of additional cucumber.

Serves 4

Harvest Pumpkin Soup

1/4	cup (1/2 stick) butter	1/8	teaspoon crushed red pepper	
1	cup chopped onion	2	(14-ounce) cans chicken broth	
1	garlic clove, minced	1	(16-ounce) can pumpkin	
1	teaspoon curry powder	1	cup evaporated skim milk or cream	
1	teaspoon salt			
1/4	teaspoon coriander			

Melt the butter in a large saucepan over medium-high heat. Add the onion and garlic. Cook until tender, stirring occasionally.

Add the curry powder, salt, coriander and red pepper. Cook for 1 minute, stirring constantly. Stir in the broth. Reduce the heat to medium-low. Simmer for 15 minutes, stirring occasionally.

Add the pumpkin and evaporated milk and mix well. Simmer for 5 minutes, stirring occasionally.

Pour the soup in batches into a blender container. Process until smooth.

Heat to serving temperature. Ladle into soup bowls. Garnish with a dollop of sour cream and sprinkle with green onion slices.

Serves 6

Baked Potato Soup

4	large baking potatoes	12	bacon slices, cooked, crumbled
2/3	cup butter	4	green onions, chopped
2/3	cup flour	3/4	teaspoon salt
6	cups milk	1/2	teaspoon pepper
1 1/4	cups shredded Cheddar cheese	1	cup sour cream

Wash the potatoes and pierce each several times with a fork.

Bake at 400 degrees for 1 hour or until tender. Let stand until cool.

Cut the potatoes lengthwise into halves. Scoop out the centers and discard the skins.

Melt the butter in a medium saucepan over low heat. Add the flour, stirring until well blended. Cook for 1 minute or until the mixture is thickened, stirring constantly.

Add the milk gradually, stirring until well blended. Cook over medium heat until the mixture comes to a boil, stirring constantly.

Add the potatoes, 1 cup of the cheese, 1/2 cup of the crumbled bacon, 2 tablespoons of the green onions, salt and pepper and mix well.

Cook until heated to serving temperature, stirring occasionally.

Stir in the sour cream until well blended. Add additional milk if necessary for desired consistency.

Ladle into soup bowls. Top with the remaining cheese, bacon and green onions.

Serves 10

Fiesta Fruit Salad

3 cups watermelon cubes	3/4 cup chopped fresh cilantro
1 cup cantaloupe cubes	1 1/2 jalapeños, seeded, minced
1 cup honeydew melon cubes	1/4 cup fresh lime juice
3/4 cup chopped red onion	

Combine the watermelon, cantaloupe, honeydew, onion, cilantro and jalapeños in a bowl.

Add the lime juice and mix lightly. Chill, covered, in the refrigerator.

May chop the fruit into smaller pieces and serve as a fruit salsa. Add a mango if desired.

The salsa is excellent served with chicken, grilled fish or crab cakes.

Serves 8

Poppy Seed Fruit Salad Dressing

1/3 cup white or apple cider vinegar	1/2 teaspoon salt
2/3 cup sugar	1 cup vegetable oil
1 teaspoon dry mustard	1 small onion, grated
	1 1/2 teaspoons poppy seeds

Combine the vinegar, sugar, dry mustard and salt in a blender container. Process until blended.

Add the oil gradually, processing constantly until well blended. Add the onion and poppy seeds.

Refrigerate, covered, until well chilled. Serve on fruit salads or mixed fruit and greens. It is especially nice on Waldorf-type salads.

Makes 2 cups

Broccoli Crunch Salad

1	pound fresh broccoli florets	1/2	cup raisins
8	ounces bacon, crisp-cooked, crumbled	1	cup mayonnaise
3	green onions, chopped	1/4	cup sugar
1	cup shelled sunflower seeds	2	tablespoons apple cider vinegar

Break the broccoli florets into small pieces and place in a salad bowl.

Add the bacon, green onions, sunflower seeds and raisins and toss lightly to mix.

Mix the mayonnaise, sugar and vinegar in a small bowl. Add the mayonnaise mixture to the broccoli mixture just before serving and toss lightly.

May steam or microwave the broccoli until tender-crisp before mixing into the salad. Be sure to drain well.

Serves 6

Artichoke and Rice Salad

1	(6-ounce) package seasoned rice for chicken	2	(6-ounce) jars marinated artichoke hearts
4	green onions, thinly sliced	1/3	cup mayonnaise
1/2	green bell pepper, chopped	3/4	teaspoon curry powder
12	pimento-stuffed olives, sliced		

Cook the rice mix according to the package directions. Place in a large bowl. Let stand until cool.

Add the green onions, green pepper and olives and mix lightly.

Drain the artichoke hearts, reserving the marinade. Slice the artichokes and add to the rice mixture.

Place half the artichoke marinade in a bowl. Add the mayonnaise and curry powder and mix well with a whisk. Whisk in enough of the remaining artichoke marinade to make the dressing of the desired consistency. Add to the rice mixture and mix lightly.

Refrigerate, covered, until serving time.

Serves 8

Black Bean and Corn Salad

1½ (16-ounce) cans black beans	5 tablespoons olive oil
1 red bell pepper	3 tablespoons lemon juice
2 ripe plum tomatoes	5 tablespoons chopped cilantro
4 green onions with tops	¾ teaspoon salt
1 cup frozen white corn, thawed	1 teaspoon pepper

Drain and rinse the beans under cool running water and drain well.

Seed and chop the red bell pepper. Seed and chop the tomatoes. Slice the green onions thinly.

Combine the black beans, red pepper, tomatoes, green onions and corn in a large bowl.

Whisk the olive oil, lemon juice, cilantro, salt and pepper in a bowl until well blended.

Add to the black bean mixture and toss lightly to mix.

Cover and let stand at room temperature for 1 hour or longer before serving. Salad may be served at room temperature or chilled.

Store any leftover salad in the refrigerator.

Serves 6

The Graves House on Rivermont Avenue was built for William E. Graves and his family in 1902. The house remained in the Graves family for several generations and, when it was sold in the 1980s, became the headquarters of the **Junior League of Lynchburg.** Family members still live nearby in residences that were originally the property's stable and a schoolhouse that was built by Mr. Graves for the purpose of educating neighborhood children. Designed by Aubrey Chesterman, the Georgian Revival-style house features ionic pilasters and elaborate exterior detailing. The widow's walk affords an unrestricted view of the surrounding neighborhoods. Each time a firetruck screamed along Rivermont Avenue, the Graves children reportedly raced to the top of the house to spot the fire's location.

Foo Mi Slaw

2 tablespoons butter
1 package ramen noodles
4 to 6 tablespoons slivered almonds
4 to 6 tablespoons sesame seeds
4 to 6 green onions, chopped
1 medium red cabbage, shredded
1/2 cup Miracle Whip or mayonnaise
1/4 cup sugar
1/4 cup red wine vinegar

Melt the butter in small skillet over medium-low heat. Add the noodles and almonds. Cook until very lightly browned, stirring frequently. Add the sesame seeds. Cook until golden brown, stirring frequently. Drain the mixture on paper towels.

Combine the green onions and cabbage in a large bowl. Add the toasted noodle mixture and toss lightly.

Combine the salad dressing, sugar and vinegar in a bowl and whisk until blended. Add to the cabbage mixture and mix lightly.

Serves 6 to 8

Marinated Cole Slaw

A favorite from *Good Cookin' from the Heart of Virginia*

1 medium cabbage, shredded
1 green bell pepper, finely chopped
1 red onion, finely chopped
3/4 cup sugar
2/3 cup vegetable oil
1 cup vinegar
1/2 cup sugar
1 teaspoon salt
1 teaspoon celery seeds
1 teaspoon dry mustard

Combine the cabbage, green pepper and onion in a large bowl and toss lightly to mix. Pour 3/4 cup of the sugar over the cabbage mixture; do not stir.

Combine the oil, vinegar, 1/2 cup sugar, salt, celery seeds and dry mustard in a saucepan. Bring to a boil, stirring until the sugar dissolves. Pour the hot mixture over the cabbage mixture and toss lightly.

Refrigerate, covered, overnight. The salad will keep for 2 to 3 weeks in the refrigerator and stay fresh and crisp.

Serves 12 to 14

Goat Cheese Medallions over Baby Greens

1	(4-ounce) cylindrical package goat cheese		3	cups mixed baby greens
1	egg		1	medium ripe tomato, cut into wedges
¼	cup shredded Parmesan cheese		¼	cup chopped red onion Favorite vinaigrette dressing
¼	cup bread crumbs			
2	tablespoons unsalted butter or olive oil			

Place the goat cheese in the freezer for several minutes before slicing; it must be very cold to slice well. Cut the cheese into six ½-inch slices.

Beat the egg in a shallow dish. Combine the Parmesan cheese and bread crumbs in another shallow dish or on waxed paper.

Dip the cheese slices into the egg, then into the bread crumb mixture, turning to coat evenly on both sides.

Melt the butter in a small skillet. Add the cheese slices. Cook until golden brown on both sides, turning once. Drain on paper towels.

Arrange the greens on 2 salad plates. Top with the tomato and onion. Arrange 3 cheese slices on each salad. Drizzle your favorite vinaigrette dressing over the entire salad.

Serves 2

Greek Pita Pockets

A favorite from *Good Cookin' from the Heart of Virginia*

8	ounces feta cheese, cubed	3	tablespoons vegetable oil
2	medium tomatoes, chopped	1	tablespoon fresh lemon juice
1	large cucumber, peeled, chopped	1	teaspoon oregano
			Salt and pepper to taste
1	small red onion, thinly sliced	4	pita bread rounds
		8	lettuce leaves
1/4	cup sliced black olives (optional)		Alfalfa sprouts (optional)

Combine the cheese, tomatoes, cucumber, onion and olives in a large bowl and toss lightly to mix.

Whisk the oil, lemon juice, oregano, salt and pepper in a bowl until well blended. Add to the cheese mixture and toss lightly.

Cut the pita rounds crosswise into halves and open to form pockets. Place a lettuce leaf in each pita pocket. Fill with the salad. Add alfalfa sprouts.

Serves 4

Layered Party Salad

1	head cauliflower	2	cups mayonnaise
1	head lettuce	1/3	cup grated Parmesan cheese
1	red onion, chopped	1/4	cup sugar
1	pound bacon slices, crisp-cooked, crumbled		

Cut or break the cauliflower into florets and tear the lettuce into bite-size pieces.

Layer the cauliflower, lettuce, onion and bacon in a large deep salad or trifle bowl.

Combine the mayonnaise, Parmesan cheese and sugar in a bowl and mix until well blended.

Spread the mayonnaise mixture over the salad, sealing to the edge. Refrigerate, covered, for several hours to overnight.

Toss the salad just before serving.

Serves 12

Hearts of Palm Salad

1	(14-ounce) can hearts of palm, drained	2	to 3 heads Bibb lettuce Basil and Garlic Salad Dressing
1	red or yellow bell pepper, cut into thin strips		
1/2	pint cherry tomatoes, cut into halves		

Cut the hearts of palm into 1/2-inch slices.

Combine the hearts of palm, red pepper and cherry tomatoes in a bowl and mix lightly.

Arrange the lettuce leaves on individual salad plates. Top with the hearts of palm mixture.

Drizzle the Basil and Garlic Salad Dressing over the salad.

Serves 6

Basil and Garlic Salad Dressing

1/4	cup balsamic vinegar	1/8	teaspoon salt
2	tablespoons lemon juice	1/8	teaspoon pepper
4	fresh basil leaves	1/3	cup olive oil
1	large garlic clove		

Combine the vinegar, lemon juice, basil, garlic, salt and pepper in a blender container. Process until well blended.

Add the olive oil gradually, processing constantly to mix well.

May prepare the dressing ahead and refrigerate, covered, until ready to serve, but the dressing should be processed again just before serving to mix the ingredients.

Tomato and Green Bean Salad

2	pounds fresh green beans, trimmed	1/4	cup chopped fresh basil
8	large tomatoes, cut into wedges	1/2	cup olive oil
8	ounces feta cheese, crumbled	3	tablespoons white wine vinegar
3/4	cup pitted kalamata olives	1	teaspoon salt
1/4	cup chopped green onions	2	teaspoons pepper

Cook the beans in boiling water in a saucepan for 5 to 6 minutes or until tender-crisp. Drain and rinse with cold water to stop the cooking process. Drain well and place in a large bowl. Add the tomatoes, cheese, olives, green onions and basil and mix lightly.

Whisk the olive oil, vinegar, salt and pepper in a bowl until well blended. Add to the bean mixture, tossing lightly. Refrigerate, covered, for 6 to 12 hours.

Serves 12

Mixed Greens with Sunflower Seeds

1	tablespoon Dijon mustard	1	cucumber, peeled, cut into thin slices
1/4	cup red wine vinegar	1	yellow bell pepper, julienned, cut into halves
1	tablespoon chopped parsley		
1 1/2	teaspoons sugar	20	to 30 seedless red grapes, cut into halves
1/2	teaspoon salt		
1/2	teaspoon pepper	3	to 4 ounces goat cheese, crumbled
1/2	cup olive oil		
1	head Boston lettuce	1/2	(3.75-ounce) package shelled sunflower seeds
1	head romaine		
1	large carrot, sliced		

Combine the Dijon mustard, vinegar, parsley, sugar, salt and pepper in a bowl and mix well. Add the olive oil gradually, whisking constantly until blended.

Tear the Boston lettuce and romaine into bite-size pieces. Place the greens, carrot, cucumber, yellow pepper and grapes in a large bowl and toss lightly. Sprinkle with the cheese.

Drizzle the desired amount of the dressing over the salad and toss to coat. Sprinkle with the sunflower seeds. Store any remaining dressing in the refrigerator.

Serves 8

Orange and Romaine Salad

1 head romaine
1 red onion, thinly sliced
1 or 2 avocados, peeled, sliced
1 (11-ounce) can mandarin oranges, drained
8 ounces fresh mushrooms, sliced
8 ounces feta cheese, crumbled
1 (2-ounce) package sliced almonds
Croutons (optional)
Feisty Salad Dressing

Tear the romaine into bite-size pieces. Combine the romaine, onion, avocado, oranges, mushrooms, cheese, almonds and croutons in a large bowl and toss lightly.

Drizzle the desired amount of Feisty Salad Dressing over the top and toss lightly. Serve immediately.

Serves 6 to 8

Feisty Salad Dressing

7 tablespoons olive oil
3 to 4 tablespoons balsamic vinegar
2 tablespoons honey
$1/2$ teaspoon ground cumin
Salt and pepper to taste
Chopped fresh basil, oregano, tarragon or minced garlic (optional)

Combine the olive oil, vinegar, honey, cumin, salt, pepper and basil in a jar with a tight-fitting lid. Shake until well blended.

Refrigerate, covered, until ready to use. Bring to room temperature before serving with the salad.

Makes about 3/4 cup

Fair by the James is a four-day event held in Lynchburg each Memorial Day weekend. It is presented by Lynch's Landing in conjunction with Atlantic Rural Exposition, Inc., a non-profit organization that also presents the annual State Fair of Virginia. The Fair brings together residents from across the region and has the feel of a state fair with its livestock displays and contests. Fair by the James also features musical performances, rides for all ages, exhibitions, concessions, and nightly fireworks displays. Situated on the banks of the James River, the Fair by the James emphasizes the revitalization of Lynchburg's riverfront.

Japanese Noodle Salad

8	ounces vermicelli	1/4	cup soy sauce
1/3	cup sesame seeds	1/4	cup hot water
1	bunch broccoli	2	tablespoons white wine or
1/4	cup chopped green onions		fruit juice
1/4	cup vegetable oil	2	teaspoons sugar

Cook the vermicelli in a large saucepan of boiling water according to the package directions. Drain and place in a large bowl.

Toast the sesame seeds in a small skillet over high heat until lightly browned and aromatic, stirring frequently. Add to the vermicelli and toss lightly.

Cut or break the florets from the broccoli into bite-size pieces. Peel the broccoli stems if desired and cut into small pieces.

Steam the broccoli for 3 minutes or until tender-crisp; drain. Rinse with cold water to stop the cooking process and drain well.

Add the broccoli and green onions to the vermicelli and mix lightly.

Whisk the oil, soy sauce, hot water, wine and sugar in a bowl until well blended. Add to the vermicelli mixture and mix lightly.

May add shredded or cubed chicken sautéed in olive oil until light brown to serve as a main dish salad.

Serves 4

Orzo and Shrimp Salad

1 1/2 (1-pound) packages orzo (rice-shaped pasta)
1 1/2 bunches green onions, chopped
12 ounces feta cheese
3/4 cup chopped fresh dill
7 tablespoons fresh lemon juice
6 tablespoons olive oil
3 pounds peeled medium shrimp
Salt and pepper to taste
2 cucumbers
2 pints cherry tomatoes, cut into halves

Cook the orzo in a large saucepan of boiling water for about 10 minutes or until just tender. Drain and rinse with cold water to cool. Drain well and place in a large bowl. Add the green onions, feta cheese, dill, lemon juice and olive oil and mix lightly.

Cook the shrimp in a large saucepan of boiling salted water for about 3 minutes or just until the shrimp turn pink. Drain and rinse with cold water to cool. Add to the salad and mix lightly. Season with the salt and pepper.

Cut half of 1 of the cucumbers into thin slices and set aside to use for a garnish.

Cut the remaining cucumbers into quarters lengthwise and slice crosswise 1/4 inch thick. Add to the salad. Add 3/4 of the cherry tomato halves and toss lightly. Transfer the salad to a large salad bowl.

Arrange the sliced cucumbers and remaining cherry tomato halves around the edge of the bowl. Garnish with sprigs of fresh dill.

May substitute grilled marinated chicken for the shrimp.

Serves 20

Tempting Tortellini Salad

1	(16-ounce) package frozen Oriental-style vegetable mix	1	teaspoon basil
1	pound tortellini	1/2	teaspoon oregano
1/3	cup olive oil	1/2	teaspoon garlic powder
1/4	cup wine vinegar	3/4	teaspoon salt
2	tablespoons lemon juice	1/8	teaspoon pepper
2	teaspoons prepared mustard	1/2	cup grated Parmesan cheese

Place the frozen vegetables in a colander. Cook the tortellini in boiling water in a large saucepan according to the package directions. Pour the tortellini with the cooking water over the vegetables in the colander; drain well.

Place the tortellini and vegetables in a large bowl and toss to mix lightly.

Whisk the olive oil, vinegar, lemon juice, mustard, basil, oregano, garlic powder, salt and pepper in a bowl until well blended. Add to the tortellini mixture and toss lightly. Sprinkle with the Parmesan cheese.

Serve warm, at room temperature or refrigerate, covered, for 2 hours or until chilled.

Serves 6

Brandy Slushies

4	regular-size tea bags		2	(12-ounce) cans frozen orange juice concentrate, thawed
2	cups boiling water			
2	cups sugar			
7	cups cold water		2	cups brandy
2	(12-ounce) cans frozen lemonade concentrate, thawed			Lemon-lime soda

Place the tea bags in a tea pot or medium bowl. Pour the boiling water over the tea bags and steep for 5 minutes. Remove and discard the tea bags. Set the tea aside to cool.

Combine the sugar and cold water in a medium saucepan. Bring to a boil, stirring until the sugar is dissolved. Let stand until cool.

Pour the tea, sugar mixture, lemonade concentrate, orange juice concentrate and brandy into a freezer-proof container and stir until well blended.

Freeze, covered, until firm.

Spoon about 1/2 cup frozen tea mixture into a tall glass for each serving. Add 1/2 cup soda and stir until slushy.

May store the slush mixture, covered, in the freezer for several weeks. Recipe ingredients may be cut in half.

Serves 30

Merry Margaritas

1	(12-ounce) can frozen limeade concentrate, thawed		3/4	limeade can tequila (about 9 ounces)
1 1/2	limeade cans water (about 18 ounces)			Coarse salt (optional)
3/4	limeade can Triple Sec (about 9 ounces)			Crushed ice

Combine the limeade concentrate, water, Triple Sec and tequila in a pitcher and mix well. Sprinkle a generous amount of salt on a plate or waxed paper. Moisten glass rims and dip the rims into the salt to coat. Add crushed ice to the glasses and fill with Margarita mixture. Garnish with lime wedges.

Serves 10 to 12

Catalpa Breeze

1/4 cup cranberry juice
1 1/4 ounces (2 1/2 tablespoons) Citron Absolut Vodka
1/4 ounce (3/4 tablespoon) Rose's lime juice

1/4 ounce (3/4 tablespoon) Triple Sec or Cointreau
1 cup ice cubes

Combine the cranberry juice, vodka, lime juice and Triple Sec in a cocktail shaker.

Add the ice cubes and shake well. Strain the juice mixture into 2 chilled martini glasses. Garnish each glass with a lime twist.

Serves 2

Celebration Punch

1 (28-ounce) bottle club soda, chilled
1 (750-milliliter) bottle champagne, chilled
1 jigger (1 1/2 ounces or 3 tablespoons) brandy
1 jigger (1 1/2 ounces or 3 tablespoons) orange liqueur

1 jigger (1 1/2 ounces or 3 tablespoons) cherry liqueur
2 oranges
2 lemons
Maraschino cherries, drained (optional)

Combine the club soda, champagne, brandy and liqueurs in a punch bowl and stir gently.

Slice the oranges and lemons thinly, discard the seeds. Float the slices on top of the punch for decoration. Add the cherries. Place the punch bowl in a larger container filled with shaved ice to keep chilled.

Serves 12

"Peaches Are In" Daiquiris

A favorite from *Good Cookin' from the Heart of Virginia*

6	ripe peaches, peeled and sliced, or 1 (16-ounce) package frozen sliced peaches, thawed	1	(6-ounce) can frozen limeade concentrate
1	cup light rum	1/4	teaspoon almond extract
		6	cups crushed ice

Combine the peaches, rum, limeade concentrate and almond extract in a blender container and process until well blended.

Add the ice and process until smooth. Pour into chilled glasses.

Serves 6

White Sangria

3 1/2	cups white wine		Coarsely chopped apples
1/2	cup Triple Sec		Chopped seedless oranges
1/4	cup sugar	1	(12-ounce) can club soda

Combine the wine, Triple Sec and sugar in a large pitcher and stir until the sugar dissolves.

Refrigerate, covered, overnight or longer. Add the fruit at any time and chill until serving time. Stir in the club soda just before serving.

Serves 4

Long Island Iced Tea

1 1/2 ounces (3 tablespoons) Triple Sec
1/4 cup cola
1/4 cup sweet-and-sour mix
1 ounce (2 tablespoons) tequila

1 ounce (2 tablespoons) gin
1 ounce (2 tablespoons) vodka
1 ounce (2 tablespoons) rum
Ice cubes or crushed ice

Combine the Triple Sec, cola, sweet-and-sour mix, tequila, gin, vodka and rum in a pitcher and stir gently.

Pour into tall ice-filled glasses.

Serves 1 or 2

Bill's Limeade Tea

4 family-size tea bags (regular or decaffeinated)
1 1/2 cups boiling water
1 (6-ounce) can frozen limeade concentrate, thawed

1/2 to 3/4 cup sugar
Ice cubes or crushed ice

Place the tea bags in a pitcher or teapot. Pour the boiling water over the tea bags and let steep for 5 minutes; discard the tea bags. Pour the brewed tea into a 2-quart pitcher.

Stir in the limeade concentrate and sugar. Add enough cold water to fill the pitcher. Pour into tall ice-filled glasses.

Serves 6 to 8

Bread & Breakfast

Favorite Apple Coffee Cake

1/3	cup packed brown sugar	1/2	cup (1 stick) margarine, softened
1	teaspoon cinnamon		
1/2	cup chopped pecans	1 1/2	cups flour
3 1/2	large yellow apples, peeled	1	teaspoon baking soda
1	cup sugar	1	teaspoon salt
1	egg		

Combine the brown sugar, cinnamon and pecans in a food processor container. Process until the mixture is well mixed and the pecans are finely chopped. Set the mixture aside.

Chop the apples coarsely. Place the apples, sugar, egg, margarine, flour, baking soda and salt in the food processor container. Process until the mixture is well mixed.

Spoon the batter into a greased 8-inch round cake pan. Sprinkle with the brown sugar topping.

Bake at 350 degrees for 60 minutes or until a wooden pick inserted in the center comes out clean.

Cool the coffee cake in the pan or serve warm.

Serves 10

Photograph on overleaf:
Rose Garden
by Max Eckert
courtesy of Veranda

Committee Coffee Cake

½ cup (1 stick) butter, softened	1 cup sour cream
1 cup sugar	1 teaspoon vanilla extract
2 eggs	⅓ cup packed brown sugar
2 cups sifted flour	¼ cup sugar
1 teaspoon baking powder	1 teaspoon cinnamon
1 teaspoon baking soda	1 cup chopped pecans
½ teaspoon salt	

Cream the butter and 1 cup sugar in a large mixer bowl until light and fluffy. Add the eggs 1 at a time, mixing well after each addition.

Sift the flour, baking powder, baking soda and salt together. Add to the creamed mixture alternately with the sour cream, mixing well after each addition. Blend in the vanilla.

Combine the brown sugar, ¼ cup sugar and cinnamon in a bowl and mix well. Stir in the pecans.

Spoon half the batter into a greased and floured bundt pan, tube pan or 9x13-inch cake pan. Sprinkle with half the brown sugar mixture. Cover with the remaining batter. Sprinkle with the remaining brown sugar mixture.

Bake at 350 degrees for 35 to 40 minutes or until the coffee cake tests done.

Cool in the pan for 10 minutes. Invert onto a serving plate. Cool completely.

Serves 15

The view from a bedroom window reveals a garden resplendent with old brick and roses, a popular southern pair. The blend of old garden and modern roses and pre-Civil-War brick recalls the past while offering a glorious morning view full of promise for the future. Old garden roses, such as 'Rosa Mundi' and 'Hansa', are those that were in cultivation prior to 1867. Modern hybrid teas, such as 'Sonia', 'Medallion', and 'Mister Lincoln', are also prominent features in a formal garden. The pre-Civil-War brick in this residential garden came from the ruins of Islington, an Amherst County house.

Blueberry and Sausage Breakfast Cake

1	pound turkey sausage	¼	cup packed brown sugar
2	cups flour	2	eggs
1	teaspoon baking powder	1	cup sour cream
½	teaspoon baking soda	1	cup blueberries
½	cup (1 stick) margarine, softened	½	cup chopped pecans
			Blueberry Sauce
¾	cup sugar		

Cook the sausage in a large skillet until brown and crumbly, stirring frequently. Drain well and set aside.

Combine the flour, baking powder and baking soda in a bowl and stir until well mixed.

Cream the margarine, sugar and brown sugar in a large mixer bowl until light and fluffy. Add the eggs 1 at a time, beating for 1 minute after each addition.

Add the flour mixture alternately with the sour cream, mixing well after each addition. Fold in the sausage and blueberries gently.

Spread the batter evenly in a greased 9x13-inch baking pan. Sprinkle with the pecans.

Bake at 350 degrees for 35 to 40 minutes or until golden brown. Cut into squares and serve warm with Blueberry Sauce.

Serves 12

Blueberry Sauce

2	cups sugar	8	cups blueberries
½	cup cornstarch	2	teaspoons lemon juice
2	cups water		

Combine the sugar and cornstarch in a large saucepan. Stir in the water gradually. Cook over medium heat until the sugar and cornstarch dissolve completely, stirring constantly.

Add the blueberries and mix well. Cook until the sauce comes to a boil and is thickened, stirring constantly.

Remove from the heat and stir in the lemon juice.

Blueberry Buckle

$1/4$	cup Crisco shortening		2	cups blueberries
$3/4$	cup sugar		$1/2$	cup sugar
1	egg		$1/3$	cup flour
$1/2$	cup milk		$1/2$	teaspoon cinnamon
2	cups sifted flour		$1/4$	cup ($1/2$ stick) butter,
2	teaspoons baking powder			softened
$1/2$	teaspoon salt			

Cream the shortening and $3/4$ cup sugar in a large mixer bowl until light and fluffy. Add the egg and mix well. Blend in the milk.

Sift 2 cups flour, baking powder and salt together. Add to the creamed mixture and mix well. Fold in the blueberries gently.

Spread the batter evenly in a greased and floured 9-inch square cake pan.

Combine $1/2$ cup sugar, $1/3$ cup flour and cinnamon in a bowl and mix well. Cut in the butter until crumbly. Sprinkle over the cake batter.

Bake for 45 to 50 minutes or until a wooden pick inserted in the center comes out clean.

Cool the buckle in the pan or serve warm.

Serves 8 to 10

Cranberry Bread

2	cups sifted flour	1	egg
1	cup sugar	3/4	cup orange juice
1/2	teaspoon salt	3	tablespoons melted butter
1/2	teaspoon baking powder	1	cup cranberries, sliced
1/2	teaspoon baking soda	1	cup chopped pecans

Combine the flour, sugar, salt, baking powder and baking soda in a medium bowl and mix well.

Whisk the egg in a small bowl. Add the orange juice and butter and whisk until well blended.

Add the egg mixture to the flour mixture and stir just until mixed.

Fold in the cranberries and pecans gently.

Pour the batter into a greased 5x9-inch loaf pan.

Bake at 350 degrees for 1 hour or until the bread tests done.

Cool the bread in the pan for 10 minutes. Remove to a wire rack to cool completely.

This bread is especially good toasted and buttered as a breakfast treat.

Serves 12

Irish Soda Bread

4	cups flour	1/4	cup (1/2 stick) butter	
1/4	cup sugar	1	egg	
1	teaspoon baking powder	1 1/3	cups buttermilk	
1	teaspoon salt	1	teaspoon baking soda	
2	tablespoons caraway seeds	1	egg yolk, beaten	

Combine the flour, sugar, baking powder, salt and caraway seeds in a large bowl. Cut in the butter until crumbly.

Whisk the egg in a small bowl. Add the buttermilk and baking soda and whisk until well blended.

Add the egg mixture to the flour mixture and mix well until the mixture forms a ball.

Place the dough on a lightly floured surface and knead until smooth and shiny. Shape the dough into a ball. Place on a greased baking sheet.

Cut a slit across the top of the dough with a sharp knife and brush with the beaten egg yolk.

Bake at 375 degrees for 1 hour or until the crust is golden brown and the bread tests done. Remove to a wire rack to cool.

Serves 6 to 8

The Legacy Museum *of African-American history is located at 403 Monroe Street, adjacent to the Old City Cemetery. Architect Edward G. Frye designed the Victorian structure with its intricate exterior detailing. Legacy participates in the ongoing revitalization of the downtown Tinbridge neighborhood. The museum will house collections of local African-American memorabilia, as well as mount exhibitions and present programs that emphasize the African-American contributions to education, religion, the arts, medicine, and civil rights.*

Zucchini Bread-in-a-Can

3   cups flour
1   teaspoon baking powder
1   teaspoon baking soda
1   teaspoon salt
1   tablespoon cinnamon
2   cups shredded zucchini

1   cup chopped pecans
3   eggs
1   cup vegetable oil
2   teaspoons vanilla extract
2   cups sugar

Combine the flour, baking powder, baking soda, salt and cinnamon in a bowl and mix well. Stir in the zucchini and pecans.

Beat the eggs, vegetable oil and vanilla in a large mixer bowl until well blended. Add the sugar and mix well.

Add the flour mixture and mix just until moistened. Spoon the batter evenly into 3 greased and floured clean 1-pound coffee cans.

Bake at 350 degrees for 55 to 60 minutes or until a wooden pick inserted in the centers comes out clean.

Cool in the cans for 10 minutes. Remove from the cans to wire racks to cool completely.

May bake the bread in 3 loaf pans instead of the coffee cans. Bake as directed.

Wrap the loaves in plastic wrap and add colorful bows. The loaves make perfect Christmas gifts for teachers or neighbors.

Serves 36

Banana Chocolate Chip Muffins

½ cup (1 stick) butter, softened	2 cups flour
¾ cup sugar	1 teaspoon baking soda
2 eggs	1 teaspoon salt
1 cup mashed very ripe bananas	¾ cup miniature semisweet chocolate chips
1 teaspoon vanilla extract	

Cream the butter and sugar in a large mixer bowl until light and fluffy.

Add the eggs 1 at a time, mixing well after each addition. Add the bananas and vanilla and mix until smooth.

Combine the flour, baking soda and salt in a bowl. Add to the creamed mixture and stir just until moistened; batter will be lumpy.

Stir in the chocolate chips; do not overmix.

Spoon the batter into paper-lined muffin cups, filling each cup ⅔ full.

Bake at 350 degrees for 25 minutes or until the muffins are golden brown and test done.

Serves 12

The **Old City Cemetery**, also known as the Old Methodist Cemetery, was founded in 1806 on land donated by city founder John Lynch. The approximately 25,000 citizens who are buried in the cemetery represent the city's diverse history. In the cemetery's Confederate Section are the graves of more than 2,000 soldiers from 14 states who died in the Lynchburg hospitals during the Civil War. The Old City Cemetery also features the Pest House Medical Museum and the Cemetery Center for orientation and research. Self-guided tours encourage visitors to learn about the cemetery's African-American history, gravestones, and nineteenth-century horticulture, including the extensive collection of antique roses. The cemetery is on the Virginia Landmarks Register and the National Register of Historic Places.

Cream Cheese Bran Muffins

2½ cups flour	⅓ cup raisins
2 cups sugar	2 eggs
2½ teaspoons baking soda	2 cups buttermilk
½ teaspoon salt	½ cup vegetable oil
1 tablespoon cinnamon	Cream Cheese Filling
3½ cups Raisin Bran	

Sift the flour, sugar, baking soda, salt and cinnamon into a large bowl. Stir in the Raisin Bran and raisins.

Whisk the eggs, buttermilk and oil in a bowl until well blended. Add to the flour mixture and stir just until moistened.

Spoon 1 tablespoon of the batter into each of 24 paper-lined muffin cups. Spoon 2 teaspoons of the Cream Cheese Filling over the batter in each muffin cup. Top each with 1 tablespoon or more of the remaining batter, spreading to cover the filling.

Bake at 400 degrees for 20 minutes or until the muffins test done. Remove to wire racks to cool.

May refrigerate the batter, covered, for up to 1 week.

Makes 24 muffins

Cream Cheese Filling

8 ounces cream cheese, softened	2 tablespoons flour
⅓ cup sugar	1 teaspoon vanilla extract

Combine the cream cheese, sugar, flour and vanilla in a bowl and mix well. May refrigerate, covered, for up to 1 week.

Refrigerator Bran Muffins

1 cup Bran Buds or other whole bran cereal	2 cups buttermilk
1 cup hot water	2½ cups flour
¼ cup (½ stick) margarine, softened	2 cups Bran Flakes
1½ cups sugar	1½ teaspoons baking soda
2 eggs, beaten	1 teaspoon salt
	½ to 1 cup raisins

Combine the Bran Buds and hot water in a bowl. Let stand for 30 minutes.

Cream the margarine and sugar in a large mixer bowl until light and fluffy. Beat in the eggs and buttermilk.

Combine the flour, Bran Flakes, baking soda and salt in a bowl and mix well. Add to the creamed mixture and stir just until moistened. Stir in the Bran Buds mixture and raisins. Refrigerate, covered, for 8 to 10 hours.

Spoon the batter into paper-lined muffin cups, filling each cup ⅔ full.

Bake at 375 degrees for 15 to 18 minutes or until the muffins test done.

May store the batter, covered, in the refrigerator for up to 6 weeks.

Editor's Note: If you intend to hold the batter for more than a day or two, we recommend substituting pasteurized egg substitute for the whole fresh eggs.

May substitute your favorite fruit for the raisins.

Makes about 4 dozen muffins

Orange Blossom Muffins

1	egg	1/2	cup chopped pecans
1/2	cup orange juice	1/2	cup sugar
1/4	cup sugar	1 1/2	tablespoons flour
1	tablespoon vegetable oil	1/2	teaspoon cinnamon
2	cups baking mix	1/4	teaspoon nutmeg
1/2	cup orange marmalade	1	tablespoon margarine

Beat the egg, orange juice, 1/4 cup sugar and oil in a mixer bowl until well blended. Add the baking mix and beat for 30 seconds. Stir in the marmalade and pecans gently.

Spoon the batter into 12 paper-lined muffin cups, filling each cup 2/3 full.

Combine 1/2 cup sugar, flour, cinnamon and nutmeg in a medium bowl and mix well. Cut in the margarine until crumbly. Sprinkle over the muffin batter.

Bake at 350 degrees for 20 minutes or until the muffins test done. Remove to a wire rack to cool or serve warm.

Serves 12

Sister Sue's No-Fuss Sticky Buns

1/2	cup chopped pecans	1/2	cup packed brown sugar
1	(24-count) package frozen roll dough	1	tablespoon cinnamon
1	(4-ounce) package vanilla pudding and pie filling mix	1/2	cup (1 stick) butter, melted

Sprinkle the pecans over the bottom of a greased bundt pan. Arrange the roll dough over the pecans.

Combine the pudding mix, brown sugar and cinnamon in a bowl and stir until well mixed. Sprinkle over the roll dough. Drizzle with the butter.

Cover the pan with a clean dish towel. Let stand for 10 to 12 hours.

Bake at 350 degrees for 30 minutes or until the bread tests done. Cool in the pan for 10 minutes. Invert onto a wire rack to cool completely or onto a serving plate to serve warm.

Serves 8

Hearty Breakfast

2	potatoes	8		eggs, lightly beaten
8	ounces bacon, chopped			Salt and pepper to taste
1	onion, thinly sliced	1/8		teaspoon nutmeg

Scrub the potatoes. Place in a saucepan and add enough water to cover potatoes. Cook over high heat just until tender. Drain and set aside to cool completely.

Peel the potatoes and cut into small cubes. Set aside.

Cook the bacon in a large skillet over medium heat until crisp, stirring frequently. Remove the bacon to paper towels to drain. Drain the skillet, reserving the drippings. Return 3 tablespoons of the reserved drippings to the skillet.

Add the onions to the drippings in the skillet. Cook until tender, stirring occasionally.

Add the potatoes. Cook until the potatoes are tender and lightly browned, stirring occasionally and adding additional bacon drippings to the skillet if the potatoes start to stick.

Add the eggs and bacon. Cook until the eggs are set, stirring constantly.

Season with salt, pepper and nutmeg and serve immediately.

Serves 6

Montview was originally the home of Senator Carter Glass, the "father of the Federal Reserve System." The modified Georgian Revival- style mansion was built in 1923 and is located on property that is now a part of **Liberty University**, formerly known as Liberty Baptist College. The Reverend Jerry Falwell founded the private Baptist university located on 160 acres of Candler's Mountain. The campus once functioned as pastureland to Glass' prize-winning Jersey cattle. Glass inscribed the motto, "A bottle of milk is a bottle of health," on each of the Montview Dairy milk bottles.

Houseguest Breakfast Casserole

1 pound bulk pork sausage	$^{1}/_{2}$ teaspoon salt
10 eggs	$1^{1}/_{2}$ cups shredded Cheddar cheese
$2^{1}/_{4}$ cups milk	
$1^{1}/_{2}$ teaspoons dry mustard	3 slices white bread, cubed

Cook the sausage in a large skillet until brown and crumbly, stirring frequently; drain well.

Beat the eggs, milk, dry mustard and salt in a mixer bowl for 1 minute.

Add the sausage, Cheddar cheese and bread to the egg mixture and stir until mixed thoroughly.

Pour the mixture into an ungreased 9x13-inch baking pan.

Bake at 350 degrees for 30 to 40 minutes or until a knife inserted in the center comes out clean.

May assemble the casserole as directed and refrigerate, covered, overnight.

Bake, uncovered, for 40 to 50 minutes or until a knife inserted in the center comes out clean.

May use any flavor pork sausage to your taste.

Serves 12

Impossible Quiche

1	pound spicy bulk pork sausage	1/2	cup frozen chopped broccoli, partially thawed
2	tablespoons butter	2	cups shredded Swiss cheese
1/2	cup chopped onion	1	cup baking mix
1/2	cup chopped green bell pepper	2	cups milk
1/2	cup sliced mushrooms	4	eggs
1/2	cup slivered almonds		Pepper to taste

Cook the sausage in a large skillet until brown and crumbly, stirring frequently; drain. Pour the drippings from the skillet.

Add the butter to the skillet. Heat until melted. Add the onion, green pepper, mushrooms and almonds. Cook until the vegetables are tender, stirring frequently; drain well.

Spoon the mixture evenly into a 10-inch quiche dish. Sprinkle with the broccoli, sausage and Swiss cheese.

Combine the baking mix, milk, eggs and pepper in a blender container. Process for 15 seconds or until smooth and well blended. Pour evenly over the ingredients in the quiche dish.

Bake at 400 degrees for 35 to 40 minutes or until a knife inserted halfway between the center and outside edge comes out clean. Let stand for 5 minutes before serving.

May substitute chopped cooked chicken or crisply cooked bacon for the cooked sausage, or frozen chopped spinach for the broccoli.

Serves 6

Sausage Quiche

1	cup cooked bulk pork sausage		1	tablespoon Grey Poupon mustard
1	unbaked (9-inch) pie shell		1	tablespoon minced onion
1	cup shredded Cheddar cheese		1/4	teaspoon salt
3	eggs		1/4	teaspoon pepper
1	cup whipping cream or half-and-half			

Spread the sausage evenly over the bottom of the pie shell.

Sprinkle the Cheddar cheese evenly over the sausage.

Whisk the eggs, whipping cream, Grey Poupon mustard, onion, salt and pepper in a bowl until well blended.

Pour the egg mixture over the cheese and sausage.

Bake at 350 degrees for 35 to 40 minutes or until a knife inserted in the center comes out clean.

May substitute the desired amount of cooked shrimp, lobster, bacon, ham or crab meat for the sausage.

Serves 6 to 8

Sausage and Wild Rice Casserole

2	pounds bulk pork sausage	1	cup sliced fresh mushrooms
1	(6-ounce) package Uncle Ben's long grain and wild rice	1	cup chopped celery
		1	cup chopped onion
¾	cup barley	2	(10-ounce) cans cream of chicken soup

Cook the sausage in a large skillet until brown and crumbly, stirring frequently; drain well.

Cook the rice according to the package directions.

Cook the barley according to the package directions.

Combine the cooked rice and barley in a large bowl and mix well.

Stir in the sausage, mushrooms, celery and onion. Add the soup and mix well. Spoon the mixture into a buttered 3-quart baking dish.

Bake at 350 degrees for 45 minutes.

May assemble and bake the casserole as directed and freeze, tightly wrapped. Thaw the casserole in the refrigerator and bake, uncovered, at 350 degrees for 45 minutes or until heated through.

This casserole is good as an addition to a brunch buffet.

Serves 8 to 10

Avoca, a 1901 Altavista house is built on the property originally owned and occupied by Colonel Charles Lynch. Lynch's father received the land in 1740 as part of a land grant from King Charles II. The original dwelling, Green Level, was home to the Lynch family for over 100 years. Avoca was built over the foundations of that dwelling, which burned in 1879, and a second one, which burned in 1899. Lynchburg architect John Minor Botts Lewis designed Avoca, which typifies the Queen Anne style popular in the early 1900s. Avoca is owned by the town of Altavista. It is on the National Register of Historic Places and is a Virginia Historic Landmark.

Easy Cheese Strata

12	slices white bread	1/4	cup (1/2 stick) margarine, melted
1	pound sharp Cheddar cheese, shredded	1	(4-ounce) can chopped green chiles (optional)
6	eggs		
2	cups milk		

Remove and discard the crusts from the bread. Cube the bread and scatter evenly over the bottom of a greased 9x13-inch baking dish.

Sprinkle the Cheddar cheese evenly over the bread.

Whisk the eggs, milk and margarine in a bowl until well blended.

Drain the green chiles and stir into the egg mixture. Pour over the ingredients in the baking pan.

Refrigerate, covered, overnight.

Bake, uncovered, at 375 degrees for 35 minutes or until a knife inserted in the center comes out clean.

May add the desired amount of cooked sausage, bacon or other meat to the cheese strata for an even heartier dish.

Serves 6 to 8

Accessories

Steamed Asparagus with Balsamic Shallots

1	large bunch fresh asparagus	$^1/_3$	cup balsamic vinegar
2	tablespoons olive oil	$1^1/_2$	tablespoons capers
2	shallots, minced	3	tablespoons grated Parmesan
2	garlic cloves, minced		cheese

Snap the tough ends from the asparagus and discard. Peel the large asparagus spears if necessary.

Place the spears in a steamer basket over boiling water in a large saucepan.

Steam, covered, for 3 to 5 minutes or just until the asparagus is tender-crisp. Keep warm.

Heat the olive oil in a large saucepan over medium-high heat. Add the shallots and garlic. Cook until tender, stirring occasionally. Reduce the heat to medium.

Add the vinegar and capers. Simmer until the liquid is thickened, stirring frequently. Stir in the Parmesan cheese.

Place the asparagus on a serving plate. Spoon the sauce over the asparagus.

Serves 4

Photograph on overleaf:
Pharsalia
by Robert DeVaul

Baked Bean Quintet

6	slices bacon	1	(15-ounce) can red kidney beans, drained
1	cup chopped onion	³/₄	cup ketchup
1	garlic clove, minced	¹/₂	cup molasses
1	(19-ounce) can chick-peas, drained	¹/₄	cup packed brown sugar
1	(17-ounce) can lima beans, drained	1	tablespoon Worcestershire sauce
1	(16-ounce) can butter beans, drained	1	tablespoon prepared mustard
1	(15-ounce) can pork and beans	¹/₄	teaspoon pepper

Cook the bacon in a large skillet over medium heat until crisp. Remove the bacon to paper towels to drain. Reserve the drippings in the skillet. Crumble the bacon.

Add the onion and garlic to the drippings in the skillet. Cook until tender, stirring occasionally. Remove the onion and garlic with a slotted spoon to a large bowl. Add the crumbled bacon and mix well.

Stir the chick-peas, lima beans, butter beans, pork and beans and kidney beans into the bacon mixture. Add the ketchup, molasses, brown sugar, Worcestershire sauce, mustard and pepper and mix well. Pour into a lightly greased 2¹/₂-quart bean pot or baking dish.

Bake, covered, at 375 degrees for 1 hour.

Serves 8 to 10

*A July hailstorm in central Virginia during the early 1960s caused damage to many of the local crops. Area orchards, like Silver Creek on the **Pharsalia Farm**, an orchard in the nearby community of Tyro, had plenty of fruit on the trees. However, the cosmetic damage to the apples prevented bulk purchasers from accepting their orders. When Perkins Flippin of Pharsalia found herself with a large amount of slightly damaged fruit, she rented a stand near Lynchburg's Langhorne Road. That fruit stand is now* The Farm Basket, *a popular shop for purchasing everything from gifts to kitchen and garden accessories. Each fall, a festival at* The Farm Basket *offers activities for all ages, including apple-butter making.*

Indian Black Beans and Rice

1	(10-ounce) package yellow saffron rice	1	tablespoon dried cilantro, or 2 tablespoons chopped fresh cilantro
2	(16-ounce) cans black beans, drained, rinsed	2	teaspoons chili powder
6	tablespoons lime juice	2	teaspoons ground cumin

Cook the rice in a medium saucepan according to the package directions.

Combine the black beans, lime juice, cilantro, chili powder and cumin in a large saucepan. Cook over medium heat until heated through, stirring occasionally.

Spoon the rice onto a serving platter. Top with the black bean mixture.

Garnish with sour cream and chopped green onions.

Serves 6 to 8

Company Carrots

2 1/2	pounds carrots	1/4	cup crushed saltines
1/2	cup mayonnaise	1	teaspoon chopped fresh parsley
2	tablespoons prepared horseradish	1/2	teaspoon paprika
1/4	teaspoon salt		

Peel or scrape the carrots and cut into strips. Cook the carrots in water to cover in a large saucepan until tender. Drain the carrots, reserving 1/4 cup of the cooking liquid. Place the carrots in a shallow baking dish.

Combine the mayonnaise, horseradish, salt and reserved cooking liquid in a bowl and mix well. Spread over the carrots.

Combine the crushed saltines, parsley and paprika in a bowl and mix well. Sprinkle over the top of the mayonnaise mixture.

Bake at 375 degrees for 10 minutes or until lightly browned.

Serves 4 to 6

Elegant Carrot Soufflés

3	pounds carrots	1/2	cup flour
1 1/2	cups (3 sticks) butter, melted	1	tablespoon baking powder
6	eggs	1/4	teaspoon cinnamon
2 3/4	cups sugar		

Peel or scrape the carrots and cut into slices.

Cook the carrots in water to cover in a large saucepan for 15 minutes or just until tender; drain.

Place the cooked carrots in a food processor or blender container. Add the butter, eggs, sugar, flour, baking powder and cinnamon. Process until smooth.

Spoon into 2 greased 1 1/2-quart baking dishes or soufflé dishes.

Bake at 350 degrees for 1 hour or until set.

May peel, slice, cook and drain the carrots the day before. Let the carrots stand until cool. Refrigerate, covered, until ready to proceed.

Process the carrots in the food processor until smooth. Add the butter, eggs, sugar, flour, baking powder and cinnamon and process until well blended. Spoon into 2 greased 1 1/2-quart baking dishes or soufflé dishes.

Bake at 350 degrees for 1 hour or until set.

Serves 12

*Bedford's **Fancy Farm**, a Georgian-style brick home, was built in 1780 by a Scottish merchant who had come to the area to conduct business in nearby New London. The house and its gristmill were later owned by Robert Kelso and remained in the Kelso family for many years. The area, located at the foot of the Peaks of Otter near Bedford, is known as Kelso's Mill. During the Civil War, Union troops adopted the house as a headquarters and 45,000 Union soldiers camped on the grounds. Privately owned, Fancy Farm is on the National Register of Historic Places and is listed as a Virginia Historic Landmark.*

Portobello Mushrooms and Goat Cheese Tarts

1 1/2 cups balsamic vinegar
1 cup olive oil
2 garlic cloves, minced
  Salt and pepper to taste
6 large portobello
  mushrooms
6 ounces mozzarella cheese,
  cut into 6 slices

2 large fresh tomatoes, or
  4 plum tomatoes, cut into
  1/4-inch-thick slices
8 ounces goat cheese, crumbled
1 long thin zucchini, cut
  diagonally into 1/8-inch-
  thick slices
  Salt and pepper to taste

Pour the vinegar into a small saucepan. Simmer over medium heat for 20 minutes or until reduced to 1/2 cup. Pour into a large bowl. Add the olive oil, garlic, salt and pepper and whisk until well blended.

Remove the stems from the mushrooms and discard. Add the mushroom caps to the vinegar mixture and toss lightly to coat. Drain the mushrooms, reserving the vinaigrette. Place the mushrooms gill side up in a roasting pan.

Bake at 350 degrees for 10 to 15 minutes or until the mushrooms are tender.

Layer the mushrooms with the mozzarella cheese, tomatoes, goat cheese and zucchini. Season with salt and pepper.

Bake for 7 to 10 minutes longer or until the cheese is melted.

Drizzle with the reserved vinaigrette. Serve as a main dish over mixed greens or serve as a side dish.

Serves 6

Onion Pie

4	slices bacon	6	tablespoons nonfat dry milk powder
1	deep-dish pie shell	2	tablespoons flour
5	medium onions, sliced	1/4	teaspoon salt
2	eggs, beaten		
1/2	cup water		

Cook the bacon in a large skillet over medium heat until crisp. Remove the bacon to paper towels to drain. Reserve the drippings in the skillet. Crumble the bacon into the pie shell.

Add the onions to the drippings in the skillet. Cook until tender, stirring occasionally.

Remove the onions to paper towels to drain. Arrange the onions over the bacon in the pie shell.

Whisk the eggs and water in a bowl until well blended. Add the milk powder, flour and salt and whisk until well blended. Pour over the onions.

Bake at 375 degrees for 30 minutes or until set.

Let stand for several minutes before cutting into wedges. This will allow for cleaner cuts and more attractive servings.

This is especially delicious when served with beef.

Serves 10

Very Easy Roasted Potatoes

1/3 cup spicy mustard	6 medium red potatoes, cut
2 tablespoons olive oil	into chunks
1 garlic clove, minced	Grated Parmesan cheese
1/2 teaspoon Italian seasoning	

Combine the mustard, olive oil, garlic and Italian seasoning in a bowl and mix well.

Place the potatoes in a large bowl. Add the mustard mixture. Cover the bowl tightly with plastic wrap and shake the bowl gently to evenly coat the potatoes with the mustard mixture. Arrange the potatoes in an even layer on a lightly greased baking sheet.

Bake at 425 degrees for 30 to 35 minutes or until the potatoes are tender. Spoon the potatoes into a serving dish and sprinkle with the Parmesan cheese.

Serves 4

Mashed Potato Casserole

6 medium potatoes	1/2 cup chopped onion
2 cups sour cream	1 teaspoon salt
1 cup shredded Cheddar cheese	1/4 teaspoon pepper

Peel the potatoes and cut into pieces.

Cook the potatoes in water to cover in a large saucepan until tender; drain.

Mash the potatoes in a large bowl. Add the sour cream, Cheddar cheese, onion, salt and pepper and mix well. Spoon into a greased 2-quart baking dish.

Bake at 350 degrees for 45 minutes or until heated through and lightly browned on top.

May use an equivalent amount of new potatoes for the medium potatoes. Scrub the new potatoes well and leave unpeeled.

Serves 8

Basil Roasted Vegetables Over Couscous

2	tablespoons chopped fresh basil		1	medium red onion, cut into 8 wedges
2	tablespoons balsamic vinegar		1	medium red bell pepper, cut into 1-inch pieces
1	tablespoon extra-virgin olive oil		1	medium yellow bell pepper, cut into 1-inch pieces
1/4	teaspoon salt		3	cups hot cooked couscous
2	garlic cloves, crushed		1	(3-ounce) package basil-flavored goat cheese, crumbled
2	medium zucchini, cut into 1-inch-thick slices			
8	ounces mushrooms		1/8	teaspoon pepper

Whisk the basil, vinegar, olive oil, salt and garlic in a large bowl until well blended.

Add the zucchini, mushrooms, onion and bell peppers and toss lightly to evenly coat the vegetables with the oil mixture. Place in a shallow roasting pan.

Bake at 425 degrees for 35 minutes or until the vegetables are browned and tender, stirring occasionally.

Spoon the couscous onto a serving platter. Top with the roasted vegetables and sprinkle with the cheese. Sprinkle with the pepper. Garnish with sprigs of fresh basil.

May serve as a main dish with a Caesar salad and fresh bread. May substitute feta cheese for the goat cheese.

Serves 4

Crowning the Garlic King and Queen, wine tasting, garlic eating, and listening to live music are among the activities featured at the annual **Garlic Festival**. *The festival, which is held each fall at the Rebec Winery just north of Amherst, began soon after agricultural experts began promoting elephant garlic as a promising alternative crop for Virginia. Approximately 3,000 people attended the first Garlic Festival in 1991, but the popularity of the festival's activities, have swelled the more recent crowds to close to 20,000.*

Spinach-Stuffed Tomatoes for Eight

A favorite from *Good Cookin' from the Heart of Virginia*

2	pounds fresh spinach	8	tomatoes
6	slices bacon		Salt to taste
1/2	cup chopped onion	1	cup shredded mozzarella
1	cup sour cream		cheese

Rinse the spinach well and pat dry. Tear into bite-size pieces and set aside. Cook the bacon in a large skillet until crisp.

Remove the bacon from the skillet. Reserve 1/4 cup of the drippings in the skillet. Drain the bacon on paper towels and crumble.

Add the onion to the bacon drippings in the skillet. Cook until the onion is tender, stirring occasionally.

Stir in the spinach. Cook, covered, for 3 to 5 minutes. Remove the skillet from the heat and stir in the sour cream and the crumbled bacon.

Cut the tops off the tomatoes. Scoop out the pulp and discard. Drain the tomato shells and season lightly with salt.

Spoon the spinach mixture into the tomato shells and place in a shallow baking pan.

Bake at 350 degrees for 20 minutes. Sprinkle with the mozzarella cheese. Bake for 10 minutes longer.

Serves 8

Aunt Fannie's Baked Squash

3	pounds yellow squash	1/2	teaspoon pepper
1/4	cup (1/2 stick) butter, softened	1/4	cup bread crumbs or seasoned stuffing mix
2	eggs, lightly beaten	1/4	cup (1/2 stick) butter
1/2	cup chopped onion	1/2	cup bread crumbs or seasoned stuffing mix
1	tablespoon sugar		
1	teaspoon salt		

Cut the ends from the squash and slice or cut into chunks. Cook the squash in a small amount of water in a large saucepan until tender.

Drain the squash and place in a large bowl. Mash with a fork.

Add 1/4 cup butter, eggs, onion, sugar, salt and pepper and mix well. Stir in 1/4 cup bread crumbs.

Spoon into a lightly greased 9x13-inch baking dish.

Melt 1/4 cup butter in a small saucepan. Add 1/2 cup bread crumbs and toss lightly. Sprinkle the crumbs over the squash mixture.

Bake at 375 degrees for 1 hour.

Serves 8 to 10

Bedford's **Centerfest**, held each September, celebrates the city's history while encouraging downtown growth. Bedford was among the first of Virginia's cities selected as a Main Street City by the National Trust for Historic Preservation. Since its selection in 1985, the city has focused on attracting new merchants, as well as preserving and strengthening existing businesses. In addition to enhancing Bedford's economic base, the Main Street program strives to ensure that the downtown area is physically appealing. Centerfest's family-oriented activities, vendors, and entertainment offer opportunities for residents and visitors to enjoy the city's downtown.

Sweet Potato Smoothie

6	pounds (about 6 large) sweet potatoes		Salt and pepper to taste
2	tablespoons (or more) bourbon	2	cups pecan halves
6	tablespoons unsalted butter, softened	2	tablespoons butter
		1/2	teaspoon kosher salt
		2	tablespoons dark brown sugar

Scrub the sweet potatoes, pierce with a fork and place in a shallow baking pan. Bake at 425 degrees for 1 hour or until tender. Let stand to cool.

Peel the sweet potatoes. Reduce the oven temperature to 325 degrees.

Place half the sweet potatoes in a food processor container. Add the bourbon and 6 tablespoons of the butter. Process for 30 seconds or until smooth. Spoon into a large bowl.

Add the remaining sweet potatoes to the food processor container and process until smooth. Add to the sweet potato mixture in the bowl and mix well. Season with salt and pepper. Spoon into a 2-quart baking dish.

Spread the pecans in a shallow baking pan. Bake for 10 minutes. Place in a bowl. Add 2 tablespoons butter and kosher salt to the pecans and toss lightly. Arrange the pecans on top of the potato mixture and sprinkle with the brown sugar. Bake for 30 minutes or until heated through.

May prepare the sweet potato mixture and coated pecans up to 2 days ahead. Refrigerate the sweet potato mixture, covered, and store the pecans in a tightly covered container until ready to bake.

Serves 8 to 10

Baked Zucchini and Tomatoes

3	tablespoons butter	1	bay leaf
2	cups chopped onions		Salt and pepper to taste
1	green bell pepper, chopped	4	zucchini, cut into
1/2	cup chopped celery		1/2-inch-thick slices
3	garlic cloves, minced	1/4	cup olive oil
4	cups chopped tomatoes	3/4	cup dry bread crumbs
1/4	cup chopped fresh parsley	1/4	cup grated Parmesan
1	tablespoon chopped fresh basil, or 1 teaspoon dried basil		cheese
		1	tablespoon butter

Melt 3 tablespoons butter in a large skillet over medium heat. Add the onions, green pepper, celery and garlic. Cook until tender, stirring occasionally.

Add the tomatoes, parsley, basil, bay leaf, salt and pepper. Simmer for 30 minutes, stirring occasionally. Remove and discard the bay leaf.

Place the zucchini slices in a single layer on a baking sheet. Brush with the olive oil. Bake at 450 degrees for 8 to 10 minutes or until lightly browned.

Add to the tomato mixture. Cook for 5 minutes. Pour the mixture into a 2-quart baking dish.

Combine the bread crumbs and Parmesan cheese in a bowl and mix well. Sprinkle over the tomato mixture. Dot with 1 tablespoon butter.

Bake at 350 degrees for 25 to 30 minutes or until golden brown.

Serves 6 to 8

Fiesta Cheese Grits

4	cups whole milk	4	ounces sharp Cheddar
1/2	cup (1 stick) butter (do not use margarine)		cheese, shredded
1	cup uncooked grits	1	(11-ounce) can whole kernel corn, drained
1	egg, lightly beaten	1	cup chopped red and/or
1	teaspoon salt		green bell peppers
	Pepper to taste		Grated Parmesan cheese

Bring the milk to a boil in a medium saucepan over medium heat, stirring frequently. Add the butter and grits and mix well. Cook for 5 minutes or until the mixture is thickened, stirring occasionally. Remove the saucepan from the heat. Stir in the egg, salt and pepper. Add the Cheddar cheese and stir until melted. Stir in the corn and bell peppers. Pour into a greased 2-quart baking dish. Sprinkle with Parmesan cheese.

Bake at 350 degrees for 1 hour or until golden brown.

Makes a great accompaniment to chicken fajitas or tacos.

Serves 12 to 15

James River Rice

1/2	cup (1 stick) butter or margarine, melted	1	cup chopped fresh mushrooms
1	(14-ounce) can beef consommé	1	large onion, chopped
1	(14-ounce) can beef stock	1 1/2	cups uncooked white, brown or wild rice

Combine the butter, beef consommé, beef stock, mushrooms, onion and rice in a 2-quart baking dish.

Bake, covered, at 350 degrees for 1 hour or until the rice is tender and the liquid is absorbed.

Serve with ham, roast beef, or any meat.

Serves 6 to 8

Four-Cheese Risotto

2	tablespoons olive oil
1	medium onion, chopped (about 1/2 cup)
1	cup uncooked arborio or long-grain white rice
1	tablespoon dry white wine
3 1/2	cups chicken broth
1/2	cup ricotta cheese
1/4	cup shredded mozzarella cheese
1/4	cup crumbled bleu cheese
1/4	cup grated Parmesan cheese
1	tablespoon chopped fresh parsley or 1 teaspoon parsley flakes

Heat the olive oil in a large saucepan over medium-high heat. Add the onion. Cook for 3 to 5 minutes or until tender-crisp, stirring frequently.

Stir in the rice. Cook for 3 minutes, stirring frequently. Add the wine. Simmer until the liquid is evaporated.

Pour 1/2 cup of the chicken broth over the rice mixture. Cook until the liquid is absorbed, stirring occasionally. Add the remaining broth 1/2 cup at a time, stirring after each addition.

Cook for 15 to 20 minutes longer or until the rice is tender and the mixture is creamy.

Add the ricotta cheese, mozzarella cheese, bleu cheese and Parmesan cheese and mix well.

Spoon into a serving dish. Sprinkle with the parsley.

Serve with grilled steak.

Serves 4 to 6

Sharp Top and Flat Top, a pair of Blue Ridge mountains known as the **Peaks of Otter**, have long been popular for their accessible trails and vistas. Thomas Jefferson climbed Sharp Top (elevation 3,875), as have many residents and visitors, according to documents dating from the 1800s. The Peaks of Otter area encompasses 5,000 woodland acres, including the Peaks of Otter Lodge and lake, a visitor's center, a historic farm, trails, picnic areas, creeks, and campgrounds. A rock from Sharp Top was sent to the nation's capital during the construction of the Washington Monument. It is marked with the inscription:

From the summit of Otter
Virginia's loftiest Peak
To crown the monument
To Virginia's noblest son.

Angel Hair Flan

3	ounces angel hair pasta	1/2	teaspoon nutmeg
3	eggs or equivalent egg substitute	1/8	teaspoon dried thyme
			Salt and pepper to taste
1	cup whipping cream or half-and-half	1	cup grated Parmesan cheese

Cook the pasta according to package directions; drain well. Divide the pasta among 8 buttered 1/2-cup soufflé dishes.

Whisk the eggs, cream, nutmeg and thyme in a bowl until well blended. Season with salt and pepper. Stir in 2/3 cup of the Parmesan cheese.

Pour the mixture over the pasta. Sprinkle with the remaining 1/3 cup Parmesan cheese.

Bake at 350 degrees for 20 minutes or until set and golden brown.

Run a small knife around the edges to loosen. Unmold onto a serving plate. Serve hot.

May bake ahead of time. Let stand until cool. Refrigerate, covered, until ready to serve.

Bake at 350 degrees for 20 minutes or until heated through.

Serve the flan as a side dish with chicken or beef or as a luncheon main dish with a green salad.

Serves 8

Chunky Veggie Spaghetti

3 tablespoons vegetable oil	1 cup V-8 juice
1 pound fresh mushrooms, cut into quarters	1/4 cup grated Parmesan cheese
1 green bell pepper, chopped	1 tablespoon parsley flakes
1 zucchini, sliced	1 teaspoon oregano
3/4 cup chopped onion	1 teaspoon basil
1 rib celery, thinly sliced	1/2 teaspoon salt
2 garlic cloves, minced	1/4 teaspoon pepper
1 (16-ounce) can tomato sauce	1 bay leaf
1 (14-ounce) can tomatoes, or 3 fresh tomatoes, chopped	Hot cooked spaghetti

Heat the oil in a Dutch oven over medium-high heat. Add the mushrooms, green pepper, zucchini, onion, celery and garlic. Cook until tender, stirring occasionally.

Add the tomato sauce, undrained tomatoes, V-8 juice, Parmesan cheese, parsley flakes, oregano, basil, salt, pepper and bay leaf. Reduce the heat to low. Simmer for 1 hour, stirring occasionally. Remove and discard the bay leaf.

Serve the sauce over the spaghetti. Sprinkle with additional Parmesan cheese.

May add chopped cooked chicken to the sauce after simmering. Cook for 5 minutes longer or until the chicken is heated through.

Serves 8

Southwest Pasta

3	small fresh tomatoes	1/2	teaspoon chili powder
3	tablespoons chopped fresh cilantro	1/4	teaspoon salt
2	tablespoons extra-virgin olive oil	1/4	teaspoon black or white pepper
1	tablespoon fresh lime juice	4	ounces angel hair pasta
3	garlic cloves, minced	4	ounces goat or feta cheese, crumbled
1	jalapeño, seeded, finely chopped	2	tablespoons pine nuts, toasted (optional)

Peel the tomatoes and chop coarsely. Place the tomatoes with the juices in a large bowl.

Add the cilantro, olive oil, lime juice, garlic, jalapeño, chili powder, salt and pepper to the tomatoes and mix well. Cover and let stand at room temperature for 1 hour.

Cook the pasta in a large saucepan of boiling water until tender; drain. Place in a serving bowl.

Add a portion of the sauce to the pasta and toss lightly. Top with the remaining sauce. Sprinkle with the goat cheese and pine nuts.

Serves 2

Masterpieces

Beef Kabobs

1	pound sirloin steak	1/8	teaspoon garlic powder
1	(8-ounce) bottle French or Russian salad dressing	8	to 10 slices bacon
2	tablespoons Worcestershire sauce	1	red bell pepper
		1	green bell pepper
2	tablespoons lemon juice	2	small zucchini
1/8	teaspoon pepper	1	large onion
		8	medium fresh mushrooms

Cut the steak into 16 to 20 cubes of the desired size and place in a shallow glass dish. Combine the salad dressing, Worcestershire sauce, lemon juice, pepper and garlic powder in a bowl and blend well. Pour the marinade over the steak, turning to coat all the cubes. Marinate the steak, tightly covered, in the refrigerator for 8 to 24 hours.

Soak wooden skewers in water for about 30 minutes. Preheat charcoal or other grill if necessary.

Drain the steak and reserve the marinade. Cut the bacon slices into halves and wrap a bacon piece around each steak cube.

Discard the stem, membranes and seeds from the bell peppers and cut the peppers into chunks. Cut off and discard the ends from the zucchini and cut into chunks or thick slices. Cut the onion into quarters.

Thread the steak, pepper and zucchini chunks, onion quarters and mushrooms alternately onto skewers. Do not press bacon-wrapped steak tightly against the vegetable chunks or the bacon will not become crisp.

Arrange the skewers on the grill over hot coals, leaving space between skewers. Grill for 10 to 15 minutes or to desired doneness, turning and basting frequently with the reserved marinade.

Serves 4

Photograph on overleaf:
Formal Dining Room
by Robert DeVaul

Grilled London Broil

A favorite from *Good Cookin' from the Heart of Virginia*

1	*tablespoon sesame seeds*	1 1/2	*tablespoons Worcestershire sauce*
1	*tablespoon butter*	1	*large onion, chopped*
1/2	*cup strong-brewed coffee*	1	*London broil or chuck roast*
1/2	*cup soy sauce*		
1	*tablespoon vinegar*		

Sauté the sesame seeds in the butter in a skillet until golden brown. Add the coffee, soy sauce, vinegar and Worcestershire sauce and mix well. Stir in the onion.

Place the London broil in a shallow dish. Pour the onion mixture over the beef, allowing the marinade to flow around and under the beef.

Marinate, covered, in the refrigerator for several hours to overnight, turning occasionally.

Preheat the grill or broiler. Remove the beef from the marinade; discard the marinade. Place the beef on the grill or on the rack in a broiler pan.

Grill or broil to the desired degree of doneness, turning as necessary.

Place the beef on a large plate. Let stand, covered, for several minutes for easier slicing. Cut cross grain diagonally into thin slices.

Serves a variable number

Dining rooms are prominent features in historic homes. The gathering of the family for the day's main meal continues as a southern tradition. Many dining rooms are ornate and elaborately appointed. The food is often an extension of the decoration, as well as a source of sustenance. Thomas Jefferson's Poplar Forest is built in an octagonal shape with the dining room at the apex. Its central location in the heart of the house underscores the belief that the main meal is central to family life.

Filets Mignons with Shiitake Madeira Sauce

1   tablespoon olive oil
2   garlic cloves, minced
1/2 teaspoon freshly ground pepper

1   teaspoon dried thyme
4   (5-ounce) 1-inch beef tenderloin steaks

Combine the olive oil, garlic, pepper and thyme in a shallow dish. Add the steaks 1 at a time, turning to coat on all sides.

Preheat a large nonstick skillet over medium-high heat. Add the steaks. Cook for 10 to 15 minutes, to 160 degrees on a meat thermometer or to the desired degree of doneness, turning once.

Remove the steaks to a warm platter to keep warm. Reserve the drippings in the skillet.

Serves 4

Shiitake Madeira Sauce

8   ounces fresh shiitake mushrooms
2   shallots, finely chopped
2   garlic cloves, minced

1   cup Madeira
1/2 cup condensed beef broth
1/4 cup whipping cream

Remove the stems from the mushrooms and discard. Cut remaining caps into thin slices and set aside.

Add the shallots and garlic to the pan drippings in the skillet. Sauté the shallots and garlic in the drippings until tender.

Add the Madeira. Bring to a boil, stirring constantly. Reduce the heat to a simmer. Simmer for 10 minutes or until reduced to about 1/2 cup.

Stir in the broth and the mushrooms. Simmer for 3 minutes or until the mushrooms are tender.

Remove the skillet from the heat. Stir in the whipping cream. Spoon the sauce over the steaks. Serve immediately.

Flank Steak with Big Glo's Marinade

1	cup vegetable oil	1/4	cup chopped onion	
3/4	cup soy sauce	1	to 2 tablespoons peppercorns	
1/2	cup fresh lemon juice	2	garlic cloves	
1/4	cup prepared mustard	1	(1 1/2-pound) flank steak	
1/4	cup Worcestershire sauce			

Combine the oil, soy sauce, lemon juice, mustard, Worcestershire sauce, onion, peppercorns and garlic in a blender or food processor. Process until well mixed.

Score the flank steak diagonally in a diamond pattern, cutting about 3/4 inch deep; do not cut through the bottom.

Pour about half the marinade into a shallow container. Add the steak. Cover with the remaining marinade.

Marinate the steak, covered, in the refrigerator for 24 hours, turning the steak occasionally.

Preheat the grill. Drain the steak, discarding the marinade. Place the steak on the grill.

Grill for 20 minutes or until cooked to the desired degree of doneness, turning as necessary. Remove to a large platter. Let stand, loosely covered, for several minutes for easier slicing.

Cut the steak cross grain; angle knife slightly and cut steak into thin slices.

Serves 4

The **Virginia School of the Arts**, a residential performing arts school, attracts young talent worldwide. One of only six such high schools in the country, Lynchburg's arts school opened its doors in 1985 in the **Garland-Rodes** building on Rivermont Avenue. Stanhope Johnson designed the former public elementary school, which is noted for its intricate Beaux-arts detail. Corinthian columns grace the façade of the three-story structure named for two Confederate generals from the area. A Junior League project reconstructed the property's historic landscaping.

Tenderloins with Mustard Sauce

4	(4-ounce) beef tenderloin steaks	1/4	cup brandy
3	tablespoons coarsely ground pepper	1	tablespoon Dijon mustard
2	shallots, minced	1/3	cup heavy cream
			Salt and pepper to taste

Coat the steaks on both sides with the ground pepper. Preheat a cast-iron skillet over medium heat until very hot.

Arrange the steaks in the hot skillet. Sear for 5 minutes on each side. Place the steaks in the skillet in a preheated 350-degree oven. Bake for about 8 minutes for medium-rare or to the desired degree of doneness.

Remove the steaks to a platter and cover loosely. Reserve the pan drippings in the skillet. Place the skillet on the stovetop over low heat.

Add the shallots to the skillet. Sauté until tender. Add the brandy. Cook for about 1 minute or until the mixture is reduced to about 1 tablespoon, stirring constantly.

Stir in the mustard and cream. Bring to a simmer, stirring constantly. Season with salt and pepper.

Serve the steaks with the sauce on the side.

Serves 4

Roasted Beef Tenderloin

1	(4- to 4 1/2-pound) beef tenderloin	Salt and pepper to taste

Pat the tenderloin dry and season with salt and pepper on all sides.

Preheat the oven to 500 degrees. Place the tenderloin in an oiled roasting pan. Insert a meat thermometer into the thickest part of the tenderloin. Place the pan on the center oven rack.

Roast for 20 to 25 minutes or to 130 degrees on the meat thermometer for medium-rare.

Let the tenderloin cool to room temperature, wrap tightly and chill. Cut into thin slices. Tenderloin may be roasted up to 2 days before serving.

Serves 10 to 12

Green Pepper Steak

1	pound boneless chuck or round steak	1	cup 1-inch squares green bell pepper	
¼	cup soy sauce	2	ribs celery, thinly sliced	
1	garlic clove, minced	1	tablespoon cornstarch	
1½	teaspoons grated fresh gingerroot or ½ teaspoon ground ginger	1	cup water	
¼	cup vegetable oil	2	tomatoes, cut into wedges	
1	cup thinly sliced green onions	4	generous servings hot cooked rice	

Trim the steak and slice cross grain into ⅛-inch strips.

Combine the soy sauce, garlic and gingerroot in a bowl. Add the steak strips and toss until coated. Set aside to marinate for several minutes.

Heat the oil in a wok or large heavy skillet over high heat. Add the steak strips. Stir-fry until browned on all sides. Reduce the heat and simmer, covered, for 30 to 40 minutes or until the steak is tender, stirring occasionally.

Increase the heat to medium-high. Add the green onions, green pepper and celery. Stir-fry for about 10 minutes or until the vegetables are tender-crisp.

Dissolve the cornstarch in the water. Stir into the wok. Cook until thickened, stirring constantly.

Add the tomatoes. Heat to serving temperature or cook for several minutes until the tomatoes are tender. Serve over hot rice.

Serves 4

An inscription on the floor of the Lynchburg Regional Airport reads,

"Nothing would give me greater pleasure than to be useful to the town of Lynchburg...I consider it as the most interesting spot in the state..."

Thomas Jefferson
October 7, 1817

Fireside Beef Stroganoff

1	(1½-pound) beef fillet	8	ounces portobello
	Salt and pepper to taste		mushrooms, thinly sliced
1	tablespoon vegetable oil	½	cup dry white wine
2	tablespoons butter	⅓	cup beef broth
1	cup chopped onion	2	cups light sour cream
2	garlic cloves, minced	2	tablespoons Dijon mustard
8	ounces mushrooms, thinly	6	to 8 servings hot cooked
	sliced		egg noodles

Slice the beef cross grain into 1-inch-thick slices. Cut each slice into ⅓-inch-thick strips. Sprinkle with salt and pepper.

Heat the oil and 1 tablespoon butter in a large nonstick skillet over high heat. Add the beef strips in several batches. Sear for about 30 seconds on each side or just until browned on the outside and rare inside. Remove the beef strips to a plate as cooked.

Reduce the heat to medium. Add the remaining 1 tablespoon butter to the skillet. Add the onion and garlic and sauté until tender.

Increase the heat to medium-high. Add the mushrooms, salt and pepper. Sauté for 2 minutes. Add the wine. Bring to a boil. Boil for 3 minutes, stirring constantly.

Return the beef strips to the skillet. Stir in the broth, sour cream and Dijon mustard. Heat just to serving temperature; do not allow the sauce to boil.

Serve over the hot noodles.

Serves 6 to 8

Reuben Loaf

1	package hot roll mix	1	(8-ounce) can sauerkraut	
¼	cup Thousand Island salad dressing	4	ounces Swiss cheese, sliced	
6	ounces (or more) corned beef, thinly sliced	1	egg white, beaten Caraway seeds (optional)	

Prepare the roll mix according to the package directions up to the point at which the dough is ready for shaping.

Place the dough on a greased baking sheet and roll or pat into a rectangle.

Spread the salad dressing from end to end down the center third of the rectangle. Arrange the corned beef slices over the salad dressing layer.

Drain the sauerkraut very well. Sprinkle over the corned beef and top with a layer of the Swiss cheese.

Cut the dough on the long sides into 1-inch strips from the outer edges toward the filling using kitchen scissors or a sharp knife.

Fold the dough strips diagonally from alternating sides over the filling layers, pressing lightly to secure and moistening with a small amount of milk or water if necessary. The dough strips should enclose the filling and the loaf should resemble a braid when complete.

Cover the loaf loosely with waxed paper. Place the baking sheet over a large shallow pan half-filled with boiling water. Let rise for 15 minutes.

Remove the waxed paper. Brush the loaf with the egg white. Sprinkle with caraway seeds.

Bake at 400 degrees for 25 minutes. Let stand for several minutes for easier slicing. Cut into slices and serve warm.

Serves 6 to 8

Lazy Day Lasagna

1	pound bulk pork sausage	1	tablespoon dried parsley flakes	
1	(26- to 32-ounce) jar spaghetti sauce	1/2	teaspoon dried oregano	
1	(8-ounce) can tomato sauce	1/4	teaspoon pepper	
1	(8-ounce) package lasagna noodles	1/4	cup grated Parmesan cheese	
1	egg, lightly beaten	4	cups shredded mozzarella cheese	
1	(12- to 15-ounce) carton ricotta cheese	1	(3½-ounce) package sliced pepperoni	

Cook the sausage in a large skillet until browned, stirring until crumbly. Drain well. Stir the spaghetti sauce and tomato sauce into the sausage. Simmer until well mixed, stirring occasionally and set aside.

Cook the lasagna noodles according to the package directions, omitting the salt. Drain, rinsing with cold water to stop the cooking process. Drain well and set aside.

Combine the egg, ricotta cheese, parsley flakes, oregano, pepper and Parmesan cheese in a bowl and mix well.

Cover the bottom of a lightly greased 9x13-inch baking pan with the sauce mixture. Add layers of the noodles, ricotta cheese mixture, mozzarella cheese and remaining sauce mixture ⅓ at a time, ending with the mozzarella cheese.

Arrange the pepperoni slices on top.

Bake at 375 degrees for 30 to 40 minutes or until the sauce is bubbly and the cheese is lightly browned.

Let the lasagna stand without cutting for 10 to 15 minutes for neater serving.

Serve with a tossed salad and garlic bread.

Serves 6 to 8

Veal Marsala

1	to 2 pounds veal, sliced		3	to 4 tablespoons olive oil
1	cup flour		1/2	envelope Knorr brown gravy mix
	Salt and pepper to taste			
1	pound fresh mushrooms, sliced		1	cup water
			1/2	cup (or more) marsala
1	to 2 shallots, sliced		4	servings hot cooked rice or noodles
1	garlic clove, minced			
3	tablespoons (about) butter		1/4	cup chopped fresh parsley

Pound the veal or cut into small pieces if desired. Combine the flour, salt and pepper in a bowl and mix well. Coat the veal generously with the flour mixture and set aside.

Sauté the mushrooms, shallots and garlic in 1 tablespoon of the butter and 2 tablespoons of the olive oil in a large skillet over medium-high heat until tender. Remove the sautéed vegetables and set aside.

Add 1 tablespoon of the butter and remaining olive oil to the skillet. Add the veal. Cook for 1 minute on each side.

Combine the gravy mix and water in a jar and close tightly; shake vigorously until well mixed. Stir the gravy mixture and 1/2 cup wine into the skillet.

Increase the heat slightly. Cook for 1 minute or until the alcohol in the wine has evaporated, stirring constantly. Add additional wine if desired and cook for 1 minute longer.

Return the sautéed vegetables to the skillet. Cook over low heat for 2 to 3 minutes. Stir in the desired amount of the remaining 1 tablespoon butter to thicken slightly.

Serve over hot rice or noodles. Sprinkle with the parsley. May also serve with a favorite pasta tossed with olive oil and garlic.

Serves 4

Pork Barbecue

1	(6-pound) pork roast or fresh picnic ham	2	tablespoons fresh lemon juice
2	cups water	1/4	cup Worcestershire sauce
1	large onion, sliced	2	teaspoons prepared mustard
1	cup ketchup	2	tablepoons chili powder
1/2	cup packed brown sugar	1	onion, chopped
6	tablespoons vinegar		

Place the pork roast in a slow-cooker. Add the water and sliced onion. Cook, covered, on Low for 8 to 10 hours.

Drain the roast and discard the cooking liquid. Let stand until slightly cooled.

Remove the pork from the bone. Discard the bone and any excess fat. Chop or shred the pork and return to the slow cooker.

Combine the ketchup, brown sugar, vinegar, lemon juice, Worcestershire sauce, mustard, chili powder and chopped onion in a bowl and mix well.

Pour the mixture over the pork and mix gently.

Cook, covered, on High for 3 hours or on Low for 4 hours.

Serve the barbecue as desired.

Serves 10 to 12

Succulent Grilled Pork

2	(12-ounce) pork tenderloins	1/4	teaspoon crushed red pepper
1	(1-inch) piece fresh	1/3	cup honey
	gingerroot, peeled, minced	3	tablespoons soy sauce
1	jalapeño, seeded, minced	3	tablespoons sesame oil

Trim the tenderloins and place in a heavy sealable plastic bag.

Add the gingerroot, jalapeño, red pepper, honey, soy sauce and sesame oil. Squeeze most of the air from the bag and seal tightly. Knead gently to permit the marinade to completely coat the tenderloins.

Refrigerate for 1 hour to overnight, turning the bag and kneading gently occasionally.

Preheat the grill to medium-high heat. Drain the tenderloins, reserving the marinade.

Place the tenderloins on the grill. Grill for about 10 minutes on each side, basting frequently with the reserved marinade.

Discard any remaining marinade.

Cut the tenderloins into 1/2-inch slices and serve immediately.

Serves 4 to 6

Day in the Park, *a Junior League project since 1974, is a family-fun day in September. Attended by more than 35,000 people, the one-day event is a part of Lynchburg's Kaleidoscope, a multi-week festival showcasing the area's arts and industries. Activities include games, rides, and performances in Miller Park. Many of the booths focus on children's health or safety issues and are sponsored by non-partisan civic and professional organizations. Non-profit organizations are invited to sell concessions and participate in the* Best Concessions Contest. *This offers area agencies an opportunity to raise money while providing a variety of food offerings as well. Various corporate sponsors join the Junior League to help underwrite Day in the Park.*

Smoky White Bean Stew with Grilled Pork Tenderloin

5	vine-ripened tomatoes	2	tablespoons chopped parsley
1	large onion, chopped	1	teaspoon salt
1	rib celery, chopped	1	teaspoon white pepper
3	garlic cloves	1 1/4	pounds pork tenderloin
2	tablespoons olive oil		Salt and freshly ground
6	cups chicken broth		black pepper to taste
2	cups water	1	tablespoon melted butter
2	cups dried white beans		Sour cream

Arrange the tomatoes in a baking pan; do not allow the tomatoes to touch. Broil for about 20 minutes or until the tops are charred.

Peel the tomatoes and process in a blender or food processor until puréed.

Sauté the onion, celery and garlic in the olive oil in a 6-quart soup pot over medium-low heat until tender.

Add the tomatoes, broth, water, dried beans, parsley, salt and white pepper. Bring to a simmer. Simmer for 1 1/2 hours or until the beans are tender.

Process about 1/3 of the mixture in a blender or food processor until puréed. Stir into the soup pot. The stew may be cooled completely and then stored, covered, in the refrigerator overnight if desired.

Preheat the grill. Season the tenderloin with salt and black pepper and brush with the melted butter.

Place the tenderloin on the grill. Grill for 7 to 8 minutes or each side or until the pork is slightly pink in the center.

Slice the tenderloin lengthwise into 2 portions. Cut each portion crosswise into 1/4-inch slices.

Heat the stew to serving temperature. Place a layer of grilled tenderloin in soup bowls. Ladle hot stew on top and add a dollop of sour cream.

Serves 6

Pork Chops with Parmesan and Vermouth

4	thinly sliced pork chops	1	tablespoon olive oil
	Salt and pepper to taste	1½	cups (about) dry vermouth
1	tablespoon butter or	4	large fresh mushrooms
	margarine	¼	cup (about) Parmesan cheese

Sprinkle the pork chops with salt and pepper on both sides.

Heat the butter and olive oil in a large heavy skillet over high heat.

Arrange the pork chops in the skillet. Cook for about 2 minutes or until brown on both sides. Reduce the heat to medium.

Add enough vermouth to the skillet to almost cover the pork chops.

Slice the mushrooms as desired. Sprinkle the sliced mushrooms around the pork chops and cover the skillet immediately.

Cook for 15 to 20 minutes or until the vermouth has reduced to a sauce of the desired amount and flavor intensity.

Sprinkle generously with Parmesan cheese.

Cook, covered, until the cheese has melted completely. Serve immediately.

Serves 2 to 4

With bricks made on the property, Bedford County's **Elk Hill** was built over a five-year span beginning in 1797. Waddy Cobbs built the house down the road from St. Stephen's Episcopal Church where his brother served as the first rector. Dismount stones still stand outside the detached building, which was constructed by a later resident to house a medical practice. Although the property is privately owned, Elk Hill's 390 acres are protected by an easement to the State and National Landmark Registers.

Butterflied Lamb

1	(5- to 6-pound) leg of lamb	¼	cup raspberry vinegar
¼	cup olive oil	6	garlic cloves, minced
¼	cup Dijon mustard		

Butterfly the lamb or have your butcher butterfly the leg of lamb when purchased.

Place the lamb in a large sealable plastic bag.

Mix the olive oil, Dijon mustard, vinegar and garlic together in a small bowl. Pour into the plastic bag.

Squeeze most of the air from the bag, seal tightly and knead gently to cover the lamb with the marinade.

Marinate in the refrigerator for 1 to 2 days, turning and kneading occasionally.

Preheat the grill. Drain the lamb and discard the marinade. Place the lamb on the grill.

Grill for 15 to 20 minutes. Turn the lamb over. Grill for 15 minutes for medium-rare or longer as necessary to cook to the desired degree of doneness.

Remove the lamb to a large plate and cover loosely. Let stand for 10 to 15 minutes for easier slicing.

Cut into desired-size slices with a sharp knife.

This marinade is delicious for pork also.

Serves 10 to 12

Balsamic Chicken

1	cup vegetable oil	1	teaspoon salt
1/2	cup balsamic vinegar	1/2	teaspoon cracked pepper
3	tablespoons ketchup		Tabasco sauce to taste
3	tablespoons sugar	1	garlic clove, minced
1	tablespoon Worcestershire	2	medium scallions, chopped
	sauce	5	pounds boneless skinless
1	teaspoon dry mustard		chicken breasts

Combine the oil, vinegar, ketchup, sugar, Worcestershire sauce, dry mustard, salt, pepper and Tabasco sauce in a bowl and mix until well blended. Stir in the garlic and scallions.

Dip the chicken breasts 1 at a time in the marinade and arrange in two 9x9-inch or larger baking pans. Pour the remaining marinade over the chicken.

Marinate, covered, in the refrigerator for 6 hours to overnight.

Remove the pans from the refrigerator and let stand at room temperature for several minutes to warm slightly.

Bake at 325 degrees for 25 to 30 minutes.

Drain the chicken, reserving the marinade. Pour the marinade into a saucepan and bring to a boil.

Preheat the grill or broiler. Arrange the chicken on the grill or on a rack in a broiler pan.

Grill or broil the chicken for 3 to 5 minutes per side.

Serve the hot marinade on the side.

Serves 10 to 20

The Amazement Square Cultural Festival for Kids is a regional event held each Halloween at the museum's historic location on Lynchburg's riverfront. The hands-on activities are designed to enhance participants' understanding of the food, arts, and customs of the festival's featured countries. In addition to highlighting cultures of selected countries, the festival spotlights area schools and communities by focusing on unique aspects {of Lynchburg and the surrounding towns and counties.

Not-Quite-Barbecued Chicken

1   (3- to 4- pound) chicken
    Salt and pepper to taste
    Garlic salt

    Brown sugar
$1/4$ cup (about) melted butter

Cut the chicken into pieces as desired. Arrange the pieces in a baking pan.

Sprinkle the chicken lightly with salt and pepper and generously with garlic salt. Sprinkle generously with the brown sugar, covering the chicken well.

Drizzle enough of the melted butter carefully over the chicken pieces to moisten the brown sugar but avoid dislodging the coating.

Bake at 350 degrees for 45 minutes to 1 hour or until the chicken is tender and glazed. Serve immediately.

Serves 2 to 4

Pulled Turkey Barbecue

2   large onions, chopped
1   garlic clove, minced
2   cups cider vinegar
$1/4$ cup unsalted butter
$1/2$ cup ketchup
3   tablespoons Worcestershire
    sauce

2   tablespoons Tabasco sauce
1   tablespoon salt
1   tablespoon pepper
$1/2$ cup packed brown sugar
$1/2$ (6-ounce) can tomato paste
1   (4- to $5^{1}/_{2}$-pound) bone-in
    turkey breast

Combine the first 9 ingredients in a Dutch oven or other large heavy pan.

Bring to a simmer over medium heat, stirring until well mixed. Reduce the heat. Simmer, covered, for 15 minutes.

Place the turkey breast with the cavity side down in the sauce. Simmer, covered, for $2^{1}/_{2}$ hours or until the turkey breast is very tender.

Remove the turkey to a plate. Let stand until cool. Remove the turkey meat from the bones. Discard the bones and shred the meat.

Add the brown sugar and tomato paste to the sauce in the pan and mix well. Bring the sauce to a simmer. Add a small amount of additional tomato paste if the sauce seems dry. Return the turkey meat to the sauce in the pan and mix well. Simmer, covered, for $1^{1}/_{2}$ hours, stirring occasionally. Adjust seasonings before serving.

Serves 12

Cavatappi with Chicken, Spinach and Mushrooms

1	(10-ounce) package fresh spinach
1	tablespoon fresh lemon juice
1	teaspoon extra-virgin olive oil
1/2	teaspoon salt
1/3	teaspoon freshly ground pepper
12	ounces boneless skinless chicken breasts
1	(14-ounce) can chicken broth
1	cup heavy or whipping cream
6	teaspoons cornstarch
1/2	teaspoon salt
1/8	teaspoon pepper
3	tablespoons olive oil
1/3	cup finely chopped shallots
8	ounces mushrooms, sliced
1	pound cavatappi or other favorite pasta, cooked
1/2	cup coarsely chopped fresh parsley
1	teaspoon grated lemon zest

Rinse the spinach well, drain and pat dry. Tear the spinach leaves into small pieces and set aside.

Combine the lemon juice, 1 teaspoon olive oil, 1/2 teaspoon salt and 1/3 teaspoon ground pepper in a bowl.

Cut the chicken breasts into strips. Add to the lemon juice mixture and toss until coated. Let stand for 5 minutes.

Combine the broth, cream, cornstarch, 1/2 teaspoon salt and 1/8 teaspoon pepper in a small bowl and mix until the cornstarch dissolves. Set the mixture aside.

Heat 1 tablespoon olive oil in a large heavy skillet over high heat. Add the chicken and stir-fry until the chicken is tender. Reduce the heat to medium.

Add the remaining 2 tablespoons olive oil to the skillet. Add the shallots and mushrooms. Cook until lightly browned, stirring frequently.

Add the broth mixture and cook until the sauce thickens, stirring constantly. Add the spinach and mix well.

Add half the sauce to the cooked pasta in a large bowl. Add the parsley and lemon zest and toss to coat the pasta.

Divide the pasta among plates or pasta bowls. Top with the remaining sauce.

Serves 6

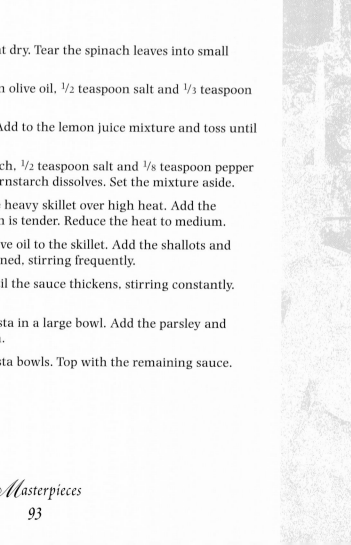

Chicken Chardonnay

1 ½	tablespoons (about) flour	¼	cup chopped onion
½	teaspoon salt	2	tablespoons chopped fresh parsley
⅛	teaspoon pepper	1	cup Chardonnay
4	large boneless skinless chicken breasts	2	cups hot cooked rice
6	tablespoons margarine	2	tablespoons chopped fresh parsley
12	to 16 ounces mushrooms, sliced		

Mix the flour, salt and pepper together. Coat the chicken with the seasoned flour; shake off the excess flour mixture and reserve.

Melt half the margarine in a large skillet over medium heat. Add the chicken. Cook the chicken until brown on both sides. Remove from the skillet.

Add the remaining 3 tablespoons margarine to the skillet. Add the mushrooms, onion and 2 tablespoons parsley. Sauté until the onion is transparent. Remove the skillet from the heat.

Sprinkle the reserved flour mixture into the skillet and mix well. Stir in the wine.

Return the skillet to the heat. Bring to a boil, stirring frequently.

Arrange the chicken in the skillet. Cover and reduce the heat to medium-low.

Simmer for 45 minutes or until the chicken is tender.

Spoon the rice onto plates. Top with a chicken breast and sauce and sprinkle with 2 tablespoons parsley. May omit the rice and serve the chicken with the sauce and a side serving of angel hair pasta with red sauce.

Serves 2 to 4

Cheesy Garlic Chicken

1	egg	4	boneless skinless chicken breasts
1	tablespoon milk		
1/2	cup grated Parmesan cheese	4	tablespoons melted butter
1	cup shredded mozzarella cheese	2	garlic cloves, crushed
			Juice of 1 lemon
1	cup herb-seasoned stuffing mix		Chopped fresh parsley to taste

Spray a baking dish with nonstick cooking spray.

Beat the egg in a medium bowl. Whisk in the milk. Add the Parmesan and mozzarella cheeses and stuffing mix and stir until well mixed and crumbly.

Roll the chicken in the mixture, patting firmly to coat well. Arrange the chicken in the baking dish.

Mix the butter and garlic together. Drizzle carefully over the chicken.

Sprinkle the chicken with lemon juice and parsley.

Bake at 350 degrees for 35 minutes or until the chicken is tender and the crust is crisp and golden brown. Serve immediately.

Serves 2 to 4

The **D-Day Memorial**, the only national memorial outside of Washington, D.C., is located on Burk's Hill in Bedford. The Memorial honors the valor, fidelity, and sacrifice of the Allied Forces who began the liberation of France on June 6, 1944. Bedford, with a wartime population of 3,200, lost 21 men on D-Day in what marked the nation's worst community loss per capita. In addition to the monument honoring the participants in Operation Overlord, the 88-acre site includes an education center. Charles M. Schulz, World War II veteran and creator of Peanuts, chairs the Memorial's national capital campaign.

Crescent Chicken Rolls

8	ounces cream cheese, softened	2	tablespoons milk
3	tablespoons melted butter	2	tablespoons minced onion
2	cups chopped cooked chicken breasts	1	tablespoon minced pimento
1/4	teaspoon salt	1	(8-count) can crescent rolls
1/8	teaspoon pepper	3/4	cup seasoned croutons
		1	tablespoon melted butter

Combine the cream cheese and 3 tablespoons melted butter in a bowl and mix until well blended.

Add the chicken, salt, pepper, milk, onion and pimento and mix well.

Separate the roll dough into 4 rectangles and press the perforations to seal.

Spoon about 1/2 cup of the chicken mixture onto the center of each rectangle.

Fold the corners of each rectangle to the center to enclose the filling, overlapping the points slightly and pressing lightly to seal.

Crush the croutons into crumbs on waxed paper. Brush the chicken rolls with the remaining tablespoon melted butter. Roll in the crushed croutons to coat and arrange on an ungreased baking sheet.

Bake at 350 degrees for 20 to 25 minutes or until golden brown and crisp. Serve immediately.

Serves 4

Crowd Control Chicken

2	cups fine soft bread crumbs		1	teaspoon pepper
½	cup grated Parmesan cheese		16	boneless skinless chicken
1	teaspoon garlic salt			breasts
½	cup chopped fresh parsley		½	cup (1 stick) butter, melted
1	teaspoon salt			Lemon Garlic Sauce

Combine the bread crumbs, cheese, garlic salt, parsley, salt and pepper in a bowl and toss until well mixed.

Dip the chicken in the melted butter and roll in the bread crumb mixture to coat well. Arrange the chicken pieces in a 9x13-inch baking pan.

Bake at 375 degrees for 15 to 20 minutes or until the chicken is almost done.

Drizzle the Lemon Garlic Sauce over the chicken.

Bake for 5 minutes longer or until the chicken is tender.

Serves 16

Lemon Garlic Sauce

½	cup (1 stick) butter		2	garlic cloves
½	cup fresh lemon juice			

Combine the butter and lemon juice in a small saucepan. Heat until the butter melts, stirring frequently.

Skewer the garlic cloves with a wooden pick. Place the garlic in the butter mixture.

Bring the mixture to a boil. Boil for 5 minutes and remove from the heat. Discard the garlic.

The **Historic Appomattox Railroad Festival** has become one of the state's largest festivals and has been recognized by the Tourism Society as one of October's top ten events in the southeastern United States. For more than a quarter of a century, participants have gathered on Main Street for music, food, games, rides, a fireman's competition, fireworks, and parades. The festival celebrates the Norfolk & Southern donation of the Appomattox Depot to the Town of Appomattox.

Feta-Stuffed Chicken Breasts

1	(10-ounce) package frozen chopped spinach, thawed		Salt and pepper to taste
8	ounces feta cheese	1/4	cup flour
1/2	cup mayonnaise	1/2	teaspoon paprika
1	garlic clove, minced	12	strips bacon
6	large boneless skinless chicken breasts		

Drain the spinach and squeeze dry. Place the spinach in a medium bowl. Crumble the feta cheese into the bowl.

Add the mayonnaise and garlic and mix well.

Cut a pocket in each chicken breast. Sprinkle with salt and pepper to taste.

Spoon the spinach mixture into the pockets. Press the pockets to close or secure with wooden picks.

Mix the flour with the paprika on waxed paper. Roll the stuffed chicken breasts in the flour mixture to lightly coat.

Wrap 2 pieces of bacon around each stuffed chicken breast.

Place a greased rack in a baking dish. Arrange the stuffed chicken breasts on the rack. Do not allow the chicken to touch.

Bake, uncovered, at 325 degrees for 1 hour or until the chicken is tender.

Serves 6

Greek Chicken Breasts

1/4	cup flour	2	medium tomatoes, peeled, chopped
1	tablespoon dried oregano	3	tablespoons sliced black olives (optional)
4	boneless skinless chicken breasts	1 1/2 to 2	tablespoons drained capers
3	tablespoons olive oil	2	tablespoons crumbled feta cheese
1/3	cup white wine		
1/3	cup chicken broth		

Mix the flour and oregano in a shallow dish or on waxed paper. Roll the chicken in the flour mixture to coat.

Heat the olive oil in a large skillet over medium heat.

Add the chicken. Cook for 10 minutes or until light golden brown on both sides, turning once.

Add the wine and broth. Simmer for 10 to 15 minutes.

Add the tomatoes, olives and capers. Cook for several minutes longer or until the sauce is heated to serving temperature.

Place the chicken in a serving dish. Spoon the sauce over the top.

Sprinkle with the feta cheese.

Serves 4

Gourmet Chicken Divan

1/3 cup flour	1 pound fresh broccoli
Freshly ground pepper to taste	2 tablespoons butter
4 boneless skinless chicken breasts	4 ounces fresh mushrooms, sliced
1/3 cup butter	1 cup sour cream
1 1/3 cups chicken broth	2 tablespoons grated Parmesan cheese
1/2 teaspoon dried basil	

Mix the flour and pepper in a shallow dish or on waxed paper. Roll the chicken in the seasoned flour to coat.

Melt the 1/3 cup butter in a large heavy skillet over medium-high heat. Add the chicken. Brown the chicken on both sides. Drain the chicken on paper towels.

Add the broth to the skillet. Cook over low heat for 5 minutes, stirring constantly to loosen the brown particles and deglaze the skillet.

Return the chicken to the skillet. Sprinkle with basil. Simmer, covered, for 30 minutes.

Rinse the broccoli well. Discard the tough stems and separate the broccoli into spears.

Cook the broccoli in a covered steamer rack over boiling water for 10 minutes or until tender-crisp. Drain and set aside.

Melt 2 tablespoons butter in a small skillet. Add the mushrooms and sauté for 2 minutes.

Arrange the broccoli spears in a buttered 9x13-inch baking dish. Remove the chicken from the skillet, reserving the drippings and arrange the chicken over the broccoli. Spoon the sautéed mushrooms over the chicken.

Blend the sour cream into the pan drippings in the skillet. Cook over low heat for several minutes until heated through; do not allow the mixture to boil.

Spoon the sauce over the chicken. Sprinkle with the Parmesan cheese.

Place the baking dish 6 inches from a preheated broiler. Broil for 3 to 5 minutes or until golden brown.

Serves 4

Lemon-Herb Grilled Chicken

1	cup vegetable oil	1	teaspoon salt
3/4	cup lemon juice	1/2	teaspoon pepper
1/4	cup honey	4	garlic cloves
2	tablespoons dried oregano	2	(3-pound) chickens
1	tablespoon dried rosemary		

Combine the oil, lemon juice, honey, oregano, rosemary, salt, pepper and garlic in a blender or food processor container. Process until smooth.

Cut the chickens into quarters and remove and discard the skins.

Place the chicken quarters in a large sealable, heavy plastic bag.

Pour the marinade into the bag. Squeeze most of the air from the bag and seal tightly. Turn the bag carefully several times to coat the chicken with the marinade.

Marinate the chicken in the refrigerator for 8 hours to overnight, turning the bag occasionally.

Preheat the grill to medium-high. Drain the chicken and discard the marinade. Arrange the chicken quarters on the grill.

Close the grill lid. Grill the chicken for 30 to 35 minutes or until the chicken is tender and brown, turning as necessary. Watch carefully to avoid burning.

May substitute boneless skinless chicken breasts for the chicken quarters and grill for an appropriate time.

Serves 8

Uncle Billy's Day *celebrates the establishment of Altavista's monthly flea market, the First Saturday Trade Lot. Town founder, W.G. Lane, known throughout the town as Uncle Billy, began the community trade lot, and the tradition has continued for nearly a century. Uncle Billy's Day is an Altavista festival dating back to 1949. The three-day celebration, held during the first weekend in June, operates in conjunction with an extended multi-day flea market and features games, crafts, concessions, exhibits, entertainment, and fireworks.*

Grilled Lime Chicken

1	cup corn oil	2	teaspoons salt
1	cup fresh lime juice		Dash of Accent
5	tablespoons chopped onion	6	boneless skinless chicken
5	teaspoons dried tarragon		breasts
1	teaspoon Tabasco sauce		

Combine the corn oil, lime juice, onion, tarragon, Tabasco sauce, salt and Accent in a medium bowl and mix well.

Reserve enough of the marinade to use for basting.

Add the chicken to the remaining marinade, turning to coat. Marinate, covered, in the refrigerator for 6 hours or longer, turning frequently.

Drain the chicken and discard the used marinade. Roll up each chicken breast and secure with wooden picks or skewers.

Preheat the grill. Arrange the chicken on the grill. Do not allow the pieces to touch.

Grill for 25 to 30 minutes or until the chicken is tender, turning and basting frequently with the reserved marinade.

Discard any remaining marinade.

Serves 6

Jazzy Jambalaya

1   onion, coarsely chopped
1   green bell pepper, coarsely chopped
3   ribs celery, coarsely chopped
2   garlic cloves, minced
2   tablespoons olive oil
8   ounces boneless chicken, cut into cubes
2   bay leaves
1/2 teaspoon thyme
1/4 teaspoon paprika
1   (28-ounce) can diced tomatoes
1/2 cup chicken stock or white wine
2   teaspoons hot sauce
1/4 cup Worcestershire sauce
1   pound smoked sausage or kielbasa
12 ounces peeled shrimp
1 1/2 cups uncooked rice
1/2 bunch green onions, chopped

Sauté the onion, green pepper, celery and garlic in the olive oil in a large heavy soup pot for 5 minutes.

Add the chicken, bay leaves and thyme. Cook over medium heat for 10 to 15 minutes or until the chicken becomes opaque, stirring frequently.

Mix in the paprika. Add the tomatoes, chicken stock, hot sauce and Worcestershire sauce and mix well.

Cut the sausage into bite-size pieces and stir into the pot. Cook until the mixture comes to a boil, stirring frequently.

Add the shrimp and rice. Cook, covered, over low heat for 30 minutes, stirring occasionally.

Ladle the jambalaya into large bowls. Sprinkle with the chopped green onions.

Jambalaya may be made with chicken only, shrimp only, a mixture of shrimp and sausage, additions of ham or crawfish or any number of other combinations.

Serves 6

Pecan-Crusted Chicken with Mustard Sauce

1	cup pecans	1	egg	
2	tablespoons cornstarch	2	tablespoons water	
1	teaspoon dried thyme	4	large boneless skinless	
1	teaspoon paprika		chicken breasts	
1 1/4	teaspoons salt	3	tablespoons vegetable oil	
1/8	teaspoon cayenne		Mustard Sauce	

Combine the pecans, cornstarch, thyme, paprika, salt and cayenne in a food processor or blender container. Pulse until the pecans are finely chopped. Pour the mixture into a shallow dish.

Whisk the egg with the water in a small bowl.

Dip each chicken breast into the egg mixture and roll in the pecan mixture to coat well.

Heat the oil in a large nonstick skillet over medium heat. Arrange the coated chicken breasts in the skillet.

Cook for 5 to 6 minutes on each side or until golden brown. Drain on paper towels and serve immediately with the Mustard Sauce for dipping.

Serves 4

Mustard Sauce

1	cup mayonnaise, sour cream or yogurt	1/2	teaspoon sugar	
2	tablespoons grainy brown mustard	1/4	teaspoon salt	
			Cayenne to taste	
1/2	teaspoon white wine vinegar	2	tablespoons chopped fresh parsley	

Combine the mayonnaise, brown mustard, vinegar, sugar and salt in a small bowl and blend well.

Stir in the cayenne and parsley.

Southwestern Chicken Pizza

1	loaf frozen white bread dough, thawed	1	(15-ounce) can black beans
2	teaspoons cornmeal	1/2	cup taco sauce
2	boneless skinless chicken breasts	3	tablespoons chopped fresh cilantro
1/4	teaspoon cumin	3/4	cup shredded Monterey Jack cheese

Divide the bread dough into 3 portions. Spray 3 small baking sheets with nonstick cooking spray and sprinkle evenly with the cornmeal.

Press or roll each portion of the bread dough into a 7-inch round on a lightly floured surface. Place 2 rounds in the center of each prepared baking sheet. If using large baking sheets that will hold more than 1 round, be sure that the rounds are not touching and have ample space to allow for expansion during the baking process.

Prick the rounds generously with a fork. Bake at 450 degrees for 8 minutes. Flatten any puffiness with a spoon. Set the partially baked crusts aside.

Cut the chicken breasts into 1/2-inch cubes.

Preheat a large skillet sprayed with nonstick cooking spray over medium heat. Add the chicken to the skillet and sprinkle with the cumin. Sauté until the chicken is no longer pink. Remove from the heat.

Drain the beans, rinse and drain well. Add the beans and taco sauce to the chicken and mix well.

Spoon the chicken mixture evenly over the partially baked crusts. Sprinkle with the cilantro and cheese.

Bake at 450 degrees for 7 to 9 minutes or until the cheese melts and the crusts are golden.

May substitute frozen pizza dough or ready-made pizza crusts for the bread dough.

Makes 3 small pizzas

*Established in 1967, **Winton Country Club** in Amherst County was originally a grand manor house built by Colonel Joseph Cabell in 1769 and named Winton after his ancestral home in England. The intricate carving in the drawing room is reputed to be the work of Hessian prisoners under Colonel Cabell's charge in the Revolutionary War. Cabell's stepson, Colonel Samuel Meredith, was a close boyhood friend and brother-in-law of Patrick Henry. Colonel Meredith lived at Winton with his wife, Jane, and her mother, Sarah Henry, until his death. They are buried in the family cemetery on the property.*

Chicken Quiche with Cheesy Pecan Crust

3	eggs	2	cups chopped cooked chicken
1/4	cup chicken broth	1/2	cup shredded Cheddar cheese
1/2	cup sour cream	1/4	cup minced onion
1/4	cup mayonnaise		Cheesy Pecan Crust
3	drops hot pepper sauce	5	pecan halves
1/4	teaspoon dried dillweed		

Beat the eggs in a medium bowl. Add the broth, sour cream, mayonnaise and hot pepper sauce and whisk until smooth and well blended.

Add the dillweed, chicken, cheese and onion and mix well. Spoon the mixture into the cooled Cheesy Pecan Crust.

Bake at 350 degrees for 30 minutes. Arrange the pecan halves decoratively in the center. Bake for 15 to 20 minutes longer or until a knife inserted in the center comes out clean.

Let stand for several minutes for easier cutting.

Serves 6

Cheesy Pecan Crust

3/4	cup flour	1/4	teaspoon salt
3/4	cup shredded Cheddar cheese	1/4	teaspoon paprika
1/2	cup chopped pecans	1/3	cup vegetable oil

Combine the flour, cheese, pecans, salt and paprika in a small bowl and mix well.

Add the oil and mix until the mixture clings together. Press the mixture evenly over the bottom and side of a 9-inch quiche pan or pie plate. Prick with a fork.

Bake at 350 degrees for 10 minutes. Let stand until cool.

Crunchy Chicken Slaw

1/4 cup slivered almonds
3 or 4 boneless skinless chicken breasts
1 head green cabbage, coarsely shredded or chopped

4 to 6 green onions, sliced
  Sesame Vinaigrette
1 package ramen noodles

Sprinkle the almonds on a piece of heavy-duty foil. Toast in a 350-degree oven for several minutes or until brown, stirring frequently. Set aside.

Cook the chicken in a small amount of simmering water for about 20 minutes or until cooked through. Drain the chicken well. Let stand until cool and shred or chop.

Combine the cabbage, chicken, green onions and toasted almonds in a large salad bowl. Add the Sesame Vinaigrette and toss to mix well.

Crumble the uncooked ramen noodles and sprinkle over the top.

Serve the salad immediately or refrigerate, covered, for several hours before serving. The salad is especially good when served wrapped in flour tortillas with a black bean and corn salad and fresh fruit.

Serves 8

Sesame Vinaigrette

1/2 cup vegetable oil
2 tablespoons sesame seed oil
6 tablespoons rice wine vinegar

3 tablespoons fresh lemon juice
3 tablespoons sugar
1 teaspoon salt
1/2 teaspoon pepper

Combine the vegetable oil, sesame seed oil, vinegar and lemon juice in a small bowl and whisk until well mixed.

Add the sugar, salt and pepper and whisk until the sugar and salt dissolve.

Grilled Chicken Salad with Asparagus

8	ounces fresh asparagus spears	2	teaspoons chopped fresh rosemary leaves
6	tablespoons olive oil, divided	1	red bell pepper
1	tablespoon lemon juice	1	yellow bell pepper
1	teaspoon Dijon mustard	1	small red onion
1/2	teaspoon salt	1/2	cup oil-pack sun-dried tomatoes
1/2	teaspoon pepper	5	ounces goat cheese, crumbled
6	to 8 boneless skinless chicken breasts	3	heads Bibb lettuce

Snap the tough ends from the asparagus. Blanch the asparagus in a large pot of boiling water for 3 minutes or until tender-crisp. Rinse immediately with cold water to stop the cooking process and drain well. Cut the asparagus spears into 1 1/2-inch pieces and set aside.

Combine 2 tablespoons of the olive oil, lemon juice, Dijon mustard, salt and pepper in a bowl and whisk until well blended. Add the chicken breasts and turn until well coated with the marinade. Refrigerate, covered, for 1 hour.

Drain the chicken and discard the marinade. Grill or pan-fry the chicken for 6 to 8 minutes on each side or until cooked through and brown. Let stand until cool.

Slice the cooled chicken into 1/4-inch-thick slices. Place the chicken slices in a large salad bowl, sprinkle with rosemary, toss to mix and set aside.

Discard the stems, seeds and membranes from the red and yellow peppers. Cut the peppers into 1 1/2-inch matchstick-size pieces.

Cut the red onion into halves. Cut each half into thin slices.

Heat 2 tablespoons of the olive oil in a large skillet over medium-high heat. Add the peppers and onion and stir-fry for about 5 minutes or until tender-crisp. Add to the chicken mixture.

Drain the sun-dried tomatoes, pat dry and chop finely. Add to the chicken mixture. Add the asparagus, goat cheese, the remaining 2 tablespoons olive oil and salt and pepper to taste. Toss until well mixed.

Separate the lettuce leaves, rinse well, pat dry and line plates with the lettuce. Spoon the salad onto the lettuce-lined plates.

Serves 6 to 8

Saturday Night Chicken

3	tablespoons dried tarragon	1/8	teaspoon pepper
1	teaspoon dried thyme	1	roasting chicken
1/4	teaspoon dried rosemary	1	onion
1	teaspoon dried sage		Celery leaves (optional)
1/2	teaspoon salt	3	lemons

Combine the tarragon, thyme, rosemary, sage, salt and pepper in a small bowl and mix well. (Double the amounts for a larger chicken.)

Rinse the chicken inside and out. Quarter the onion and insert the onion and celery leaves in the cavity.

Loosen the skin from the chicken and sprinkle the herb mixture between the skin and the meat. Replace the skin.

Place the chicken in a roasting pan. Squeeze the juice of 1 lemon over the chicken and place the lemon rinds in the chicken cavity.

Roast at 350 degrees for 1 1/2 to 2 1/2 hours or to 180 degrees on a meat thermometer, basting frequently with additional lemon juice freshly squeezed from the remaining lemons. Let stand, covered, for several minutes for easier carving.

Save the carcass of Saturday Night Chicken to make a delicious Sunday night soup.

Serves 6

The Maier Museum of Art at Randolph-Macon Woman's College houses the college's 90-year-old permanent collection of nineteenth- and twentieth-century American art. The collection represents the major phases of American art including the Hudson River School, American Impressionism, the Ashcan School, Regionalism, Abstraction, and Photo-Realism. Paintings by Gilbert Stuart, Thomas Cole, James McNeill Whistler, Winslow Homer, Mary Cassatt, George Bellows, Edward Hopper, Georgia O'Keefe, and Andrew Wyeth are among the 70 works displayed in the museum's six galleries. The museum serves the academic community as well as the general public by offering changing exhibitions, lectures, symposia, and concerts. The museum structure was built in 1952 by the National Gallery of Art in Washington, D.C. as a repository in case of national emergency.

Oriental Chicken Stir-Fry

3 1/2 tablespoons reduced-sodium soy sauce
2 tablespoons water
2 tablespoons rice vinegar
2 tablespoons oyster sauce
1 tablespoon ketchup
1 teaspoon sugar
1 garlic clove, crushed
1 cup diagonally sliced carrots
1 small yellow onion

2 tablespoons vegetable oil
1 1/2 cups diagonally sliced celery
1 cup shredded or slivered cooked chicken
1/2 cup diced red or green bell pepper
3 cups cooked rice, cooled
1 cup sugar snap peas or snow peas, stems removed

Combine the soy sauce, water, vinegar, oyster sauce, ketchup, sugar and garlic in a small bowl, mix well and set aside.

Place the carrots in a small microwave-safe dish. Add a few drops of water. Microwave, covered, for 1 minute or just until partially cooked. Set aside.

Cut the onion into thin strips. Heat the oil in a wok or large heavy skillet over medium-high heat. Add the onion to the wok. Cook until the onion begins to caramelize, stirring occasionally.

Add the celery. Stir-fry for 2 minutes. Add the carrots, chicken and bell pepper. Stir-fry for 2 minutes.

Add the rice and mix well. Add the peas. Stir in the soy sauce mixture. Heat to serving temperature, stirring frequently. Serve immediately.

Serves 4

Hilton Head Fish

A favorite from *Good Cookin' from the Heart of Virginia*

4	large flounder fillets	1/3	cup prepared mustard
1	cup mayonnaise	1/4	teaspoon garlic salt
1/4	cup dry vermouth		Salt and pepper to taste
1	tablespoon fresh lemon juice	2	medium onions, sliced
1	tablespoon Worcestershire sauce	8	ounces fresh mushrooms, sliced
3	dashes Tabasco sauce	1	teaspoon paprika

Arrange the fillets on a rack in a broiler pan. Broil for 10 to 15 minutes or until the fish flakes easily when tested with a fork. Set aside to cool.

Combine the mayonnaise, vermouth, lemon juice, Worcestershire sauce, Tabasco sauce, mustard, garlic salt and salt and pepper in a bowl and whisk until well blended.

Arrange the onion slices over the cooled fillets. Spread the mayonnaise mixture over the onions.

Add a layer of sliced mushrooms and sprinkle with paprika.

Broil for several minutes or until the mushrooms are tender and the mayonnaise mixture is golden brown.

Serves 4

Salmon Patties with Dill Sauce

1 (16-ounce) can salmon	1/4 cup chopped green bell
8 saltine crackers, crushed	pepper
1 egg, beaten	Flour
1/4 teaspoon pepper	Vegetable oil for frying
1/2 onion, chopped	Cucumber Dill Sauce

Drain the salmon and discard the skin and bones if desired. Flake the salmon in a bowl.

Add the crackers, egg, pepper, onion and green pepper to the salmon and mix until the mixture holds together.

Shape into patties of the desired size. (Small patties may be served as appetizers.)

Sprinkle flour on waxed paper. Roll the patties in flour until coated on all sides.

Heat a small amount of oil in a large heavy skillet over medium-high heat. Fry the patties in the hot oil until golden brown on both sides, turning once. Drain on paper towels.

Serve the patties hot with the Cucumber Dill Sauce.

Serves 4

Cucumber Dill Sauce

1/2 cup sour cream	Juice of 1/2 lemon
1/2 cup finely chopped cucumber	1/4 teaspoon salt
1/4 teaspoon dried dillweed	

Combine the sour cream, cucumber, dillweed, lemon juice and salt in a small bowl and mix well.

This sauce is also excellent with broiled or grilled "catch of the day."

James River Wraps

1	ounce sun-dried tomatoes	1	teaspoon minced fresh thyme	
½	cup boiling water	2	garlic cloves, crushed	
1	(8-ounce) salmon fillet		Salt and pepper to taste	
1	tablespoon chopped niçoise olives	4	(8-inch) flour tortillas	
1	tablespoon minced fresh basil	12	arugula or spinach leaves	

Combine the sun-dried tomatoes and boiling water in a small bowl. Let stand, covered, for 15 minutes or until the tomatoes are soft. Drain well and slice thinly. Set aside.

Preheat the broiler. Spray the rack of a broiler pan with nonstick cooking spray. Place the salmon on the rack. Broil for several minutes or until partially cooked.

Mix the olives, basil, thyme, garlic, salt and pepper in a small bowl. Spoon over the salmon.

Broil for about 5 minutes or until the salmon flakes easily when tested with a fork. Flake the salmon coarsely.

Warm the tortillas according to package directions.

Divide the salmon evenly among the warm tortillas. Sprinkle with the sun-dried tomatoes and cover with the arugula leaves.

Roll the tortillas up tightly to enclose the filling and place seam side down on plates. Cut crosswise into halves.

Serves 4

Queena Dillard Stovall *began her oil depictions of Virginia's rural life at the age of 63. One of twelve children, she spent her life in Lynchburg and the surrounding counties. The artist, who raised eight children, moved to a one-story house in Amherst County called* **The Wigwam** *in 1945 and lived there until her death in 1980. The home's hilltop location on Route 130 in Elon inspired many of her paintings, which typically depicted rolling hills and mountains, farm life, and everyday people engaged in everyday activities.*

Baked Crab Hampton

1/4	cup seasoned Italian bread crumbs		Dash of hot pepper sauce
1/2	cup mayonnaise	1	tablespoon chopped fresh parsley
1	teaspoon dry mustard		Salt and pepper to taste
1	tablespoon Worcestershire sauce	1	pound backfin crab meat
1	tablespoon fresh lemon juice		Seasoned Italian bread crumbs
1	tablespoon drained capers (optional)		Butter

Combine the 1/4 cup bread crumbs, mayonnaise, dry mustard, Worcestershire sauce, lemon juice, capers, hot pepper sauce, parsley, salt and pepper in a bowl and mix well.

Discard any shell pieces from the crab meat. Fold the crab meat into the mayonnaise mixture.

Spoon the mixture into a buttered 1 1/2-quart baking dish or 6 individual buttered baking shells or ramekins.

Sprinkle the desired amount of bread crumbs over the top and dot with butter.

Bake at 350 degrees for 30 minutes for the 1 1/2-quart casserole or until bubbly and the top is golden brown. Reduce the baking time for the individual containers.

This traditional recipe is good served as an accompaniment to a Virginia ham or as the main dish for lunch or dinner.

Serves 6

Boiled Lobster

6	(1½-pound) fresh Maine lobsters	3	quarts water per lobster Salt

Select a pot large enough to contain the lobsters without overcrowding. Use more than one pot if necessary. A 4-gallon pot containing 3 gallons of water is perfect for cooking 4 of the lobsters. Add ¼ cup of salt for each gallon of water to imitate the salinity of the ocean water. The lobster will be more flavorful.

Bring the water to a full rolling boil. Add the lobsters and begin timing. See the chart below. Drain the lobster. Serve with Drawn Butter (at right).

Serves 6

Steamed Lobster

6	(1½-pound) fresh Maine lobsters

The steaming method cooks the lobster more slowly than boiling, producing more tender and flavorful meat. Because it is less likely to overcook the lobster, this method will permit a few extra minutes to prepare the table for serving.

Select a 4- to 5-gallon pot for steaming 6- to 8-pounds of lobster. Place about 1-inch of salted water in the pot and add the steamer rack.

Bring the water to a boil, add the lobsters, cover tightly and begin timing. See the chart below. Rearrange the lobsters halfway through the cooking time using tongs and great care to avoid burns from the very hot steam. Drain the lobster. Serve with Drawn Butter (at right).

Serves 6

Drawn Butter

¾ cup (1½ sticks)
unsalted butter
Juice of ½ lemon
Salt and pepper
to taste

Melt the butter in a small saucepan over low heat. Add the lemon juice, salt and pepper and whisk until well mixed. Keep the butter warm over very low heat, whisking occasionally. Do not allow the butter to brown. Serve the Drawn Butter in small bowls for dipping.

Approximate Cooking Times

Size	Boiled	Steamed
1 pound	8 minutes	10 minutes
1¼ pounds	9–10 minutes	12 minutes
1½ pounds	11–12 minutes	14 minutes
1¾ pounds	12–13 minutes	16 minutes
2 pounds	15 minutes	18 minutes
2½ pounds	20 minutes	22 minutes

Jim's Oysters

6	Ritz crackers		Celery salt to taste
15	Virginia oysters with liquor		Paprika to taste
1/2	teaspoon Astor barbecue seasoning	2	tablespoons butter
	Salt and freshly ground pepper to taste	2	tablespoons half-and-half
		1	teaspoon Worcestershire sauce

Grease a 9-inch pie plate. Crush the Ritz crackers coarsely and sprinkle half the crumbs over the bottom of the pie plate.

Drain the oysters, reserving the oyster liquor. Arrange the oysters in the pie plate. Do not overcrowd; the oysters should barely touch.

Sprinkle 1 tablespoon of the reserved oyster liquor over the oysters. Sprinkle with the barbecue seasoning, salt and pepper, celery salt and paprika.

Melt the butter in a saucepan. Blend in the half-and-half and Worcestershire sauce. Spoon the mixture over the oysters to coat completely and allow the excess to flow to the bottom of the pie plate.

Sprinkle the remaining cracker crumbs over the top of the oysters.

Bake at 350 degrees for 20 minutes or until the center oysters bubble and bounce; do not overcook.

This dish is excellent prepared in individual gratin dishes for serving as appetizers.

Serves 4

Scallops Supreme

A favorite from *Good Cookin' from the Heart of Virginia*

2	pounds large fresh scallops	1/4	cup chopped green bell pepper
1/2	cup milk or light cream	2	teaspoons crushed fresh rosemary
1/4	cup Madeira or dry white wine		Salt and pepper to taste
2	teaspoons lemon juice	3/4	to 1 cup soft bread crumbs
1	teaspoon minced onion		

Arrange the scallops in a lightly greased shallow 2-quart baking dish.

Blend the milk and wine in a small bowl. Add the lemon juice, onion, green pepper, rosemary, salt and pepper. Add the bread crumbs and stir until until well mixed. Spoon evenly over the scallops.

Bake at 450 degrees for 15 minutes or until the scallops are tender.

May prepare the scallops in a microwave-safe baking dish and microwave on High for about 10 minutes or until the scallops are tender. This dish is especially good served with a favorite spinach salad.

Serves 6

Linguini and Scallops

8	ounces linguini	1	(14-ounce) can artichoke hearts, drained, cut into quarters
4	garlic cloves, minced		
1/2	cup olive oil	1	teaspoon oregano
1	pound bay scallops	2	tablespoons lemon juice
4	tomatoes, chopped	1	cup crumbled feta cheese

Cook the linguini al dente according to the package directions. Drain, rinse with hot water, drain well and place in a large bowl. Keep warm.

Sauté the garlic in olive oil in a skillet until light golden. Add the scallops. Sauté for 2 to 3 minutes or until cooked through.

Add the tomatoes, artichokes, oregano and lemon juice to the skillet. Cook until heated through, stirring occasionally. Add the sauce to the linguini and toss until coated. Crumble the feta cheese over the top.

May substitute shrimp for the scallops.

Serves 4

Shrimp Enchiladas

1	pound peeled medium shrimp	8	(6-inch) flour tortillas
1/4	teaspoon salt	1	cup shredded Monterey Jack cheese
1/8	teaspoon freshly ground pepper	1	(16-ounce) jar salsa
4	tablespoons vegetable oil	1/2	cup sour cream
1	(15-ounce) can black beans	2	teaspoons chopped fresh chives

Sprinkle the shrimp with salt and pepper. Sauté the shrimp in 1 tablespoon of the oil in a large heavy skillet over medium-high heat just until the shrimp turn pink. Remove the shrimp from the skillet.

Drain the beans, rinse and drain well. Place the tortillas on a flat surface. Spoon the beans onto half of each of the tortillas. Sprinkle the beans with cheese and arrange the shrimp on the cheese. Fold the tortillas over to enclose the filling.

Heat the remaining 3 tablespoons oil in the large skillet over medium-high heat. Arrange the filled tortillas several at a time in the skillet and fry for about 30 seconds on each side or until browned, pressing firmly to allow the cheese to melt and bond with the beans and shrimp.

Place on a paper towel-lined baking sheet to keep warm. Repeat with the remaining filled tortillas.

Pour any remaining oil from the skillet. Return 4 of the filled tortillas to the skillet. Use a second skillet for the remaining tortillas.

Divide the salsa between the skillets. Heat over medium heat for about 2 minutes or until the tortillas are slightly softened, turning once.

Place the enchiladas with the salsa on plates. Top with dollops of sour cream and sprinkle with chives.

Serves 4

Shrimp Currituck

1	pound cooked peeled shrimp	4	tablespoons butter,
	Salt and pepper to taste		softened
8	ounces fresh mushrooms,	1	tablespoon soy sauce
	sliced	1/2	cup freshly grated Parmesan
3	tablespoons butter		cheese
1	tablespoon flour		Paprika to taste
1	cup sour cream		

Arrange the shrimp in a single layer in a buttered 9x13-inch baking dish. Sprinkle with salt and pepper.

Sauté the mushrooms in 3 tablespoons butter in a large skillet until browned. Place the mushrooms in a bowl.

Sprinkle the mushrooms with flour and toss to coat lightly.

Add the sour cream and mix lightly. Add softened butter 1 tablespoon at a time, mixing gently but thoroughly after each addition.

Add the soy sauce and salt and pepper to taste and mix gently.

Spoon the mushroom mixture over the shrimp. Sprinkle with the Parmesan cheese and paprika.

Bake at 400 degrees for 10 minutes or until bubbly; do not overcook.

Serves 4 to 6

The boyhood home of **Douglas Southall Freeman**, *in downtown Lynchburg, is now occupied by local businesses. Freeman, a renowned editor and historian, graduated from the University of Richmond in 1904 and received his doctorate from Johns Hopkins University in 1908. In 1919, he received an honorary degree from Washington and Lee. From 1915 to 1949, he served as the editor of* The Richmond News Leader. *The son of a Confederate veteran, Freeman's research and writings about the Civil War distinguished him as an esteemed Civil War historian. His books on Robert E. Lee and George Washington earned him two Pulitzer Prizes. The Pulitzer for his work on Washington was awarded posthumously.*

Shrimp Mediterranean

1	(12- to 16-ounce) package tri-color rotelli	2	teaspoons dried oregano
1	teaspoon salt	1/2	teaspoon dried thyme
8	tablespoons vegetable oil	1	teaspoon black pepper
1	medium onion, minced	1/8	teaspoon crushed red pepper
2	garlic cloves, minced	12	ounces feta cheese, crumbled
1	cup dry white wine	1	(6-ounce) can sliced black olives, drained
2	(12-ounce) cans plum tomatoes	1 1/4	pounds fresh medium shrimp, peeled

Add the rotelli to a generous amount of boiling water in a large saucepan. Add the salt and 2 tablespoons of the oil to the saucepan. Cook until about three-fourths done; drain. Toss with 2 tablespoons of the oil and set aside.

Sauté the onion in 2 tablespoons of the oil in a 4-quart saucepan over medium-high heat until tender. Reduce the heat and add the garlic. Cook for 2 minutes, stirring constantly.

Stir in the wine. Reduce the heat and cook for 5 minutes, stirring occasionally.

Drain the tomatoes and cut into quarters. Add the tomatoes to the wine mixture. Cook for 10 minutes, stirring occasionally.

Add the oregano, thyme, and black and red peppers. Cook for 20 minutes, stirring occasionally. Remove from the heat.

Stir in half the feta cheese and all the olives. Set aside.

Sauté the shrimp in the remaining 2 tablespoons oil until the shrimp are about half cooked.

Add the sauce and mix well. Cook until the shrimp are completely cooked, stirring frequently.

Add the pasta and toss until heated to serving temperature.

Pour the pasta mixture into a large serving dish. Sprinkle with the remaining feta cheese. Serve immediately.

Serves 6 to 8

Spinach Linguini with Southwest Shrimp

8	ounces spinach linguini	¼	cup dry white wine
6	tablespoons butter	2	tablespoons finely chopped fresh parsley
1	tablespoon olive oil		
½	cup finely chopped shallots	2	tablespoons finely chopped fresh cilantro
1	or 2 garlic cloves, minced		
1	pound large shrimp, peeled		Dash of Tabasco sauce
1	red bell pepper		Salt and pepper to taste
3	(about) jalapeños	¼	cup freshly grated Parmesan cheese
2	tablespoons lime juice		

Cook the linguini al dente according to the package directions; drain well and set aside.

Heat the butter and olive oil in a large skillet over medium heat until the butter melts.

Add the shallots and garlic. Sauté for 2 minutes.

Add the shrimp. Sauté for about 2 minutes or just until the shrimp turn pink. Remove the shrimp to a large bowl and set aside.

Discard the stem, seeds and membrane from the red pepper and cut into matchstick-size pieces. Seed the desired number of jalapeños and chop finely.

Add the red pepper and jalapeños to the pan drippings in the large skillet over medium heat and sauté for 3 minutes or until tender.

Return the shrimp to the skillet. Add the lime juice, wine, parsley, cilantro, Tabasco sauce and salt and pepper and mix well.

Add the spinach linguini. Toss to mix well and heat to serving temperature.

Pour into a serving bowl. Sprinkle with the Parmesan cheese.

Serves 4

The historical marker at **New London Academy** *notes that it is the "oldest secondary school in the state of Virginia in continuous operation under its own charter." Among the school's many famous alumni are Thomas Jefferson's grandson and the founders of Ferrum College and the University of the South. Chartered in 1795, the school became coeducational in 1879. The school building has been used as a Bedford County elementary school since 1964.*

Southern Shrimp and Grits

1	pound shrimp, peeled	4	teaspoons fresh lemon juice
6	slices bacon		Salt and pepper to taste
	Peanut oil		Hot sauce to taste
2	cups sliced fresh mushrooms		Chopped fresh parsley to
1	cup sliced green onions		taste
1	garlic clove, crushed		Cheesy Grits

Rinse the shrimp, pat dry and set aside.

Chop the bacon into small pieces. Cook the bacon in a large heavy skillet until browned at the edges. Remove the bacon from the skillet and set aside.

Add enough peanut oil to the bacon drippings in the skillet to cover the bottom of the pan. Heat the mixture over medium-high heat.

Add the shrimp. Sauté until the shrimp begin to turn pink. Add the mushrooms, green onions, garlic and bacon.

Cook until the shrimp are pink and the bacon is crisp. Add the lemon juice, salt and pepper, hot sauce and parsley and mix well.

Divide the Cheesy Grits among 4 warm plates. Spoon the shrimp mixture over the grits and serve immediately.

Serves 4

Cheesy Grits

4	cups cooked grits	White pepper to taste
1	cup shredded sharp Cheddar cheese	Nutmeg to taste
½	cup grated Parmesan cheese	Hot sauce to taste

Prepare enough grits according to the package directions to yield the 4 cups.

Add the Cheddar and Parmesan cheeses to the hot grits and stir until the cheeses melt.

Season with white pepper, nutmeg and hot sauce, mix well and set aside. Keep the grits warm.

Finishing Touches

Chocolate Chip Pound Cake

1   (2-layer) package yellow cake mix with pudding in the mix
1   (4-ounce) package chocolate instant pudding mix
½   cup sugar
1   cup sour cream
¾   cup vegetable oil
¾   cup water
4   eggs, beaten
1   cup semisweet chocolate chips
   Sifted confectioners' sugar to taste

Combine the cake mix, pudding mix and sugar in a large bowl and stir with a wire whisk to remove any large lumps.

Add the sour cream, oil, water and eggs and whisk until well blended. Stir in the chocolate chips.

Pour the batter into a greased and floured 12-cup bundt pan.

Bake at 350 degrees for 1 hour or until a wooden pick inserted in the center comes out clean.

Cool the cake in the pan on a wire rack for 10 minutes. Invert onto a serving plate to cool completely.

Sprinkle with the confectioners' sugar.

Serves 16

Photograph on overleaf:
Living Room of Randolph-Macon Woman's College— President's Home
by Robert DeVaul

Finishing Touches

Coconut Pound Cake

1 1/2	cups (3 sticks) butter, softened		1/4	teaspoon baking soda
3	cups sugar		1	cup sour cream
6	eggs		1	teaspoon vanilla extract
3	cups flour, sifted		1	teaspoon lemon extract
1/4	teaspoon salt		1	(12-ounce) package frozen coconut

Cream the butter and sugar in a large mixer bowl until light and fluffy. Add the eggs 1 at a time, mixing well after each addition.

Sift the flour, salt and baking soda together. Add to the creamed mixture alternately with the sour cream, mixing well after each addition. Blend in the flavorings. Fold in the coconut. Pour the batter into a greased and floured tube pan.

Bake at 300 degrees for 1 1/2 hours or until the cake tests done.

Cool the cake in the pan on a wire rack for 10 minutes. Invert onto a serving plate to cool completely.

May substitute canned or packaged coconut if frozen is not available. Frozen coconut is usually not sweetened and has a texture more nearly like freshly shredded coconut.

Serves 16

The red brick residence at 3115 Rivermont Avenue is home to Kathleen Gill Bowman, eighth president of **Randolph-Macon Woman's College**, and her husband, Daniel. Randolph-Macon Woman's College purchased the Pettyjohn house in 1983, acting on the wishes of the college's trustees and members of the Lynchburg community. The Virginia Georgian home was designed by Pendleton Clark and was built in 1931. Randolph-Macon Woman's College, founded in 1891, is a selective four-year liberal arts college for women, known for its academic strength and for being the first southern women's college to earn a Phi Beta Kappa charter. The college's most famous alumna is Nobel Prize-winner Pearl S. Buck, who received her degree in 1914.

Five-Flavor Pound Cake

1	cup (2 sticks) butter, softened	1	cup milk
1½	cups Crisco shortening	1	teaspoon vanilla extract
3	cups sugar	1	teaspoon coconut extract
5	eggs	1	teaspoon lemon extract
3	cups flour	1	teaspoon rum extract
½	teaspoon baking powder	1	teaspoon butter flavoring

Cream the butter, shortening and sugar in a large mixer bowl until light and fluffy. Add the eggs 1 at a time, mixing well after each addition.

Combine the flour and baking powder in a bowl. Add to the creamed mixture alternately with the milk, mixing well after each addition. Blend in the vanilla, coconut, lemon and rum extracts and the butter flavoring. Pour the batter into a large greased and floured bundt pan.

Bake at 325 degrees for 1½ hours or until the cake tests done.

Cool the cake in the pan on a wire rack for 10 minutes. Invert the cake onto a serving plate to cool completely.

Serves 16

Sherry Cake

1	(2-layer) package yellow cake mix	¾	cup vegetable oil
1	(4-ounce) package vanilla instant pudding mix	¾	cup good quality sherry
1	teaspoon nutmeg	4	eggs
			Sherry Glaze

Combine the cake mix, pudding mix, nutmeg, oil, sherry and eggs in a large mixer bowl and beat at medium speed for 5 minutes. Pour into a greased and floured 10-inch tube pan or bundt pan.

Bake at 350 degrees for 50 to 60 minutes or until the cake tests done.

Cool the cake in the pan on a wire rack for 10 minutes. Invert onto a serving plate. Cool slightly. Drizzle the Sherry Glaze over the warm cake.

Do not use cake mix with pudding in the mix.

Serves 8 to 10

Sherry Glaze

1½ cups confectioners' sugar   ¼   cup sherry

Combine the sugar and sherry in a bowl and stir until well blended.

The **Virginia Center for the Creative Arts** (VCCA) is one of the largest residential artists' communities in the nation. Established in 1971 at Wavertree Hall near Charlottesville, the VCCA relocated to the Mt. San Angelo estate in Sweet Briar in 1978. The property originally featured an Italianate mansion from the 1850s and a 1930's Normandy-style barn. During renovations, the mansion burned to the ground and a larger residence was built. The renovated barn now houses twenty-three private studios for composers, visual artists, and writers from around the world. Residencies vary in length from one week to three months. National Book Award and Pulitzer Prize winners and nominees are among the approximately 3,000 resident artists who have come to the VCCA to concentrate on their work.

Heavenly Hummingbird Cake

3	cups flour	1½	teaspoons vanilla extract	
2	cups sugar	1	(8-ounce) can crushed	
1	teaspoon baking soda		pineapple	
1	teaspoon salt	2	cups chopped bananas	
1	teaspoon cinnamon	2	cups chopped pecans or	
3	eggs		walnuts	
1½	cups vegetable oil		Cream Cheese Frosting	

Combine the flour, sugar, baking soda, salt and cinnamon in a large bowl and mix well.

Whisk the eggs, oil and vanilla in a medium bowl until well blended. Add to the flour mixture and mix well; do not beat.

Stir in the undrained pineapple, bananas and 1 cup of the pecans. Spoon the batter evenly into three 8-inch or two 9-inch greased and floured round cake pans.

Bake at 350 degrees for 25 to 30 minutes or until the cake layers test done.

Cool the layers in the pans on wire racks for 10 minutes. Remove the layers from the pans to wire racks to cool completely.

Spread the Cream Cheese Frosting between the layers and over the top and side of the cake. Sprinkle with the remaining 1 cup chopped pecans.

Serves 12 to 14

Cream Cheese Frosting

8	ounces cream cheese, softened	1	pound confectioners' sugar
½	cup (1 stick) butter or margarine, softened	1	teaspoon vanilla extract

Beat the cream cheese and butter in a large mixer bowl until creamy.

Add the confectioners' sugar gradually, beating well after each addition. Blend in the vanilla.

Amaretto Cheesecake

1 1/2 cups chocolate wafer crumbs
1 1/3 cups blanched slivered
    almonds, toasted, chopped
1 1/3 cups sugar
6 tablespoons butter, melted
24 ounces cream cheese,
    softened

1/3 cup whipping cream
1/4 cup amaretto
1 teaspoon vanilla extract
4 eggs
    Sour Cream Topping

Combine the wafer crumbs, 1 cup of the almonds and 1/3 cup of the sugar in a bowl and mix well. Stir in the butter. Press the crumb mixture over the bottom and up the side of a 9-inch springform pan.

Combine the cream cheese and the remaining 1 cup sugar in a large mixer bowl and beat until well blended. Blend in the whipping cream, amaretto and vanilla. Add the eggs 1 at a time, mixing just until blended after each addition. Pour into the prepared springform pan.

Bake at 375 degrees for 35 minutes. Remove from the oven and cool in the pan for 10 minutes.

Spread with the Sour Cream Topping. Bake for 10 minutes longer.

Cool in the pan on a wire rack for 10 minutes. Loosen the cheesecake from the side of the pan and cool the cheesecake completely.

Refrigerate until ready to serve. Remove the side of the pan before serving. Sprinkle with the remaining 1/3 cup almonds.

Serves 12

Sour Cream Topping

2 cups sour cream
1 tablespoon sugar

1 teaspoon amaretto
1 teaspoon vanilla extract

Combine the sour cream, sugar, amaretto and vanilla in a bowl and blend well.

Deep-Dish Buttermilk Cheesecake

2	cups graham cracker crumbs	1	cup sour cream	
6	tablespoons sugar	1	tablespoon vanilla extract	
6	tablespoons melted margarine	2	cups buttermilk	
16	ounces cream cheese, softened	1	cup whipping cream	
3	cups sugar	8	eggs Berry Topping	

Combine the graham cracker crumbs, 6 tablespoons sugar and margarine in a bowl and mix well. Press evenly over the bottom of a 9- or 10-inch springform pan. Bake at 350 degrees for 10 minutes. Remove from the oven.

Beat the cream cheese and 3 cups sugar in a large mixer bowl until well blended. Add the sour cream and vanilla and mix well.

Add the buttermilk and whipping cream gradually, mixing well. Add the eggs 1 at a time, mixing just until blended after each addition. Pour into the prepared springform pan.

Bake for 35 to 40 minutes or until the cheesecake tests done.

Cool on a wire rack for 10 minutes. Loosen the cheesecake from the side of the pan; cool completely. Refrigerate until serving time.

Remove the side of the pan and place the cheesecake on a serving plate.

Cover with the Berry Topping no more than 1 hour before serving.

Serves 12 to 16

Berry Topping

2	pints strawberries	2	cups (about) confectioners' sugar
2	pints blueberries		
2	shots of brandy or to taste		

Combine the berries, brandy and confectioners' sugar in a bowl and mash until well mixed. Let stand for 2 hours.

Warm Chocolate-Filled Cheesecake

$1/2$ cup (1 stick) butter, softened
$1/3$ cup sugar
1   cup flour
1   teaspoon vanilla extract
$3/4$ cup finely chopped pistachios

32 ounces cream cheese, softened
$1 1/2$ cups sugar
4   eggs
2   teaspoons vanilla extract
2   cups semisweet chocolate chips

Cream the butter and $1/3$ cup sugar in a large mixer bowl until light and fluffy. Add the flour gradually, beating at low speed after each addition until well blended.

Stir in 1 teaspoon vanilla and the pistachios. Press the mixture over the bottom and $1 1/2$ inches up the side of a 9- or 10-inch springform pan.

Bake at 350 degrees for 15 to 20 minutes or until golden brown. Remove to a wire rack to cool.

Beat the cream cheese in a mixer bowl until light and fluffy. Add $1 1/2$ cups sugar gradually, mixing well after each addition. Add the eggs 1 at a time, mixing just until blended after each addition. Blend in 2 teaspoons vanilla.

Pour half the batter into the prepared springform pan. Sprinkle with the chocolate chips to within $1/2$ inch of the edge of pan. Pour the remaining batter over the chocolate chips, starting at the outer edge of the pan and working toward the center.

Bake at 350 degrees for 1 hour or until the center of the cheesecake is set; do not overbake. Cool in the pan on a wire rack for 30 minutes. Loosen the cheesecake from the side of the pan and cool slightly. Remove the side of the pan. Serve warm. Refrigerate leftovers.

May reheat any leftovers in the microwave just until warmed.

Serves 12

Brownies with Mint Frosting

½	cup (1 stick) butter, softened	½	teaspoon salt
1	cup sugar	½	cup chopped walnuts or
4	eggs		pecans
1	(16-ounce) can Hershey's		Mint Frosting
	chocolate syrup	6	tablespoons butter
1	teaspoon vanilla extract	1	cup chocolate chips
1	cup flour		

Cream ½ cup butter and sugar in a large mixer bowl until light and fluffy. Add the eggs 1 at a time, mixing well after each addition. Add the chocolate syrup and vanilla and mix until well blended.

Add the flour and salt and mix well. Stir in the walnuts. Pour into a greased 9x13-inch baking pan.

Bake at 350 degrees for 25 to 30 minutes or until the brownies pull from the side of the pan.

Cool in the pan on a wire rack.

Spread with the Mint Frosting. Refrigerate until chilled.

Place the 6 tablespoons butter and chocolate chips in a saucepan. Cook over medium heat until the chocolate chips and butter are melted and the mixture is smooth, stirring frequently.

Let stand until cool. Spread over the Mint Frosting. Store, covered, in the refrigerator.

Cut into squares just before serving.

Serves 15

Mint Frosting

½	cup (1 stick) butter, softened	2	tablespoons crème de menthe
2	cups confectioners' sugar		liqueur

Beat the butter in a large mixer bowl until creamy. Add the sugar gradually, beating well after each addition. Add the liqueur and mix well.

Beach Cookies

1	cup (2 sticks) margarine, softened	2	teaspoons baking powder
1	cup sugar	2	teaspoons baking soda
1	cup packed brown sugar		Pinch of salt
2	eggs	1½	cups quick-cooking oats
2	cups flour	1	cup flaked coconut
		1	cup chopped pecans

Cream the margarine, sugar and brown sugar in a large mixer bowl until light and fluffy. Add the eggs 1 at a time, mixing well after each addition.

Combine the flour, baking powder, baking soda and salt in a bowl. Add to the creamed mixture gradually, mixing well after each addition.

Stir in the oats, coconut and pecans.

Drop the dough by spoonfuls 2 inches apart onto greased cookie sheets.

Bake at 350 degrees for 10 to 15 minutes or until the cookies are light golden brown; do not overbake.

Cool on the cookie sheets for 1 minute. Remove to wire racks to cool completely.

Makes 4 to 5 dozen

The **Elks Home**, the national retirement community in Bedford for men, women, and couples who are members of the Order of the Elks, has been in operation since 1903. The sprawling facility, which was built in 1916 as a men's retirement home, combines classic and mission architecture. Over 100,000 visitors from the area ride through the winding drive to view the Christmas lights displayed each year. The Elks Home tradition began in 1953 at the direction of a resident who was a retired Barnum and Bailey artist. The original decoration of a sleigh and reindeer has evolved into a facility-wide display using over 50,000 light bulbs.

Cinnamon Twists

1	cup sour cream	3	cups flour
2	tablespoons Crisco shortening	1	egg
		2	tablespoons melted butter
3	tablespoons sugar	1/3	cup packed brown sugar
1	envelope dry yeast	1	teaspoon cinnamon
1	teaspoon salt	1	cup confectioners' sugar
1/8	teaspoon baking soda	1	teaspoon (or more) milk

Place the sour cream in a small saucepan over low heat. Heat until warmed, stirring occasionally. Remove the saucepan from the heat. Add the shortening and stir until the shortening is melted.

Add the sugar, yeast, salt and baking soda and mix until well blended. Place in a large mixer bowl. Add 2 cups of the flour and the egg. Beat at medium speed until smooth. Stir in the remaining 1 cup flour.

Place the dough on a lightly floured surface and knead for 5 minutes or until the dough is smooth and elastic. Roll the dough into an 8x24-inch rectangle and brush with the butter.

Combine the brown sugar and cinnamon in a bowl and mix well. Sprinkle evenly over the dough.

Fold the dough in half lengthwise. Cut crosswise into 1x4-inch strips. Twist the dough strips once, holding both ends of the strip as you twist. Place 2 inches apart on greased baking sheets, pressing the ends of the dough to the baking sheet to secure the twists. Cover and let rise in a warm place for 1 hour.

Bake at 375 degrees for 15 to 17 minutes or until golden brown. Remove to wire racks to cool slightly.

Place the confectioners' sugar in a bowl. Stir in enough of the milk to make glaze of the desired consistency. Drizzle over the warm twists.

Makes 24 twists

Caroline's Praline Bars

1 pound (4 sticks) butter (do not use margarine), softened	¾ cup light corn syrup
1 pound dark brown sugar	5 cups Rice Krispies cereal
¾ cup whipping cream	1½ cups chopped pecans

Combine the butter, brown sugar, whipping cream and corn syrup in a large heavy saucepan. Cook over medium heat until the mixture reaches the soft-ball stage, 238 degrees on a candy thermometer. Remove the saucepan from the heat.

Add the cereal and pecans and mix well. Pour the mixture into a 11x17-inch baking pan lined with parchment paper and spread evenly.

Let stand until cool. Cut into squares using a pizza cutter or sharp knife dipped in cold water.

Serves many

Chattanooga Chew Chews

½ cup (1 stick) butter, softened	½ cup (1 stick) butter
1 cup packed brown sugar	1 cup packed brown sugar
2 cups flour	2 cups miniature chocolate chips
1½ cups chopped pecans	

Cream ½ cup butter and 1 cup brown sugar in a large mixer bowl until well blended. Add the flour and mix well. Press the mixture evenly over the bottom of an ungreased 9x13-inch baking pan. Sprinkle with the pecans.

Combine the remaining ½ cup butter and 1 cup brown sugar in a saucepan. Bring to a boil over medium-high heat. Cook for 1 minute, stirring constantly. Pour over the pecans.

Bake at 350 degrees for 15 minutes.

Sprinkle with the chocolate chips. Let stand for 1 minute or until the chocolate chips soften. Swirl with a knife to marbleize. Cool in the pan on a wire rack. Cut into bars.

Serves 15

Smith Mountain Lake combines 5,000 woodland acres, 500 miles of shoreline, 25 marinas, three yacht clubs and a handful of specialty shops and restaurants to earn its reputation as "the jewel of the Blue Ridge." This man-made lake was a 1960s project of Appalachian Power Company (AEP). The lake now serves its original purpose as a source of hydroelectric power, as well as providing a beautiful getaway spot. Camping, hiking, golfing, and water sports, including some of the country's best bass fishing, make Smith Mountain Lake enticing to the area's more than 6,000 residents, as well as visitors from the bordering counties of Bedford, Franklin, Campbell, and Pittsylvania. Part of the lake is a designated state park, and one of the two dams welcomes passersby at its Visitors Center.

Dipped Gingersnaps

2	cups sugar	1	teaspoon salt
1½	cups vegetable oil		Sugar
2	eggs	2	(12-ounce) packages
½	cup molasses		(4 cups) vanilla baking
4	cups flour		chips
4	teaspoons baking soda	¼	cup Crisco shortening or
1	tablespoon ginger		butter
2	teaspoons cinnamon		

Combine 2 cups sugar and the oil in a large mixer bowl and beat until well blended. Add the eggs 1 at a time, mixing well after each addition. Blend in the molasses.

Combine the flour, baking soda, ginger, cinnamon and salt in a bowl and mix well. Add to the molasses mixture and beat until well blended.

Shape the dough into walnut-size balls and roll in additional sugar. Place 1 inch apart on ungreased cookie sheets.

Bake at 350 degrees for 10 to 12 minutes or until the cookies spring back when touched lightly.

Cool on cookie sheets for 1 minute. Remove to wire racks to cool completely.

Combine the baking chips and shortening in a saucepan. Cook over medium-low heat until melted, stirring frequently.

Dip the cookies one at a time into the melted vanilla chip mixture to coat only half the cookie. Let the excess coating drain and place the cookies on waxed paper. Let stand until coating is set.

May substitute chocolate chips for the vanilla chips.

Makes 13 to 14 dozen

Grandma's Molasses Cookies

3/4	cup Crisco shortening		1	teaspoon salt
1	cup sugar		1	teaspoon cinnamon
1	egg		1	teaspoon ginger
1/4	cup molasses		1	teaspoon cloves
2	cups flour		1/4	cup (or more) sugar
1	teaspoon baking soda			

Cream the shortening and 1 cup sugar in a large mixer bowl until light and fluffy. Add the egg and beat until well blended. Add the molasses and mix well.

Sift the flour, baking soda, salt, cinnamon, ginger and cloves together. Add to the molasses mixture gradually, mixing well after each addition.

Refrigerate the dough, covered, for 30 to 60 minutes or until firm enough to shape easily.

Shape the dough into 1-inch balls. Roll in 1/4 cup sugar. Place 2 inches apart on lightly greased cookie sheets.

Bake at 350 degrees for 10 minutes or until the cookies test done.

Cool on the cookie sheets for 1 minute. Remove to wire racks to cool completely.

Makes 2 to 2 1/2 dozen

Peanut Butter Oatmeal Bars

½ cup (1 stick) butter, softened	1 cup rolled oats
⅓ cup peanut butter	½ teaspoon baking soda
½ cup sugar	½ teaspoon vanilla extract
½ cup packed brown sugar	2 cups chocolate chips
1 egg	½ cup confectioners' sugar
¼ cup milk	3 tablespoons milk
1 cup flour	¼ cup peanut butter

Cream the butter, ⅓ cup peanut butter, sugar and brown sugar in a large mixer bowl until light and fluffy. Add the egg and beat until well blended. Add ¼ cup milk and mix well.

Combine the flour, oats and baking soda in a bowl and mix well. Add to the creamed mixture and beat until well mixed. Add the vanilla and mix well.

Spread the mixture evenly over the bottom of a greased 9x13-inch baking pan.

Bake at 350 degrees for 18 to 20 minutes or until golden brown.

Remove the pan from the oven. Sprinkle immediately with the chocolate chips. Let stand until softened. Spread the melted chocolate carefully to cover the baked layer completely. Place on a wire rack to cool completely.

Combine the confectioners' sugar and 3 tablespoons milk in a bowl and mix until well blended. Add ¼ cup peanut butter and mix well. Drizzle over the chocolate layer.

Let stand until firm. Cut into bars.

Makes 24 bars

White Chocolate Macadamia Nut Cookies

½ cup (1 stick) butter or margarine, softened	2 cups flour
½ cup Crisco shortening	1 teaspoon baking soda
¾ cup packed brown sugar	½ teaspoon salt
½ cup sugar	1 (6-ounce) bar white baking chocolate, cut into chunks
1 egg	1 (7-ounce) jar macadamia nuts, coarsely chopped
1½ teaspoons vanilla extract	

Cream the butter, shortening, brown sugar and sugar in a large mixer bowl until light and fluffy. Add the egg and vanilla and mix until well blended.

Combine the flour, baking soda and salt in a bowl. Add to the creamed mixture gradually, mixing well after each addition. Stir in the chocolate and macadamia nuts. Drop the dough by rounded teaspoonfuls 2 inches apart onto greased cookie sheets.

Bake at 350 degrees for 8 to 10 minutes or until lightly browned.

Cool on the cookie sheets for 1 or 2 minutes. Remove to wire racks to cool completely.

May substitute one 6-ounce package vanilla milk chips for the white chocolate baking bar or substitute chocolate chips.

Try using a small metal ice cream scoop to measure the cookie dough evenly.

Makes 5 dozen cookies

In a move that would prove to be ironic, Wilmer McLean relocated his family from their northern Virginia home in 1863. The move was precipitated by the Battles of Bull Run, which took place in Manassas, near the McLean family home. The McLeans moved to a home in the town of Appomattox Court House, never guessing that Appomattox would be the site of one of the final battles of the Civil War or that General Robert E. Lee would surrender the Army of Northern Virginia to General Ulysses S. Grant in the parlor of his family's home. **The McLean House**, located in the Appomattox Court House National Park, is open to the public.

Raspberry Shortbread

1 1/2	cups flour	3	tablespoons flour
1/2	cup sugar	1	teaspoon vanilla extract
1/2	cup (1 stick) butter, chilled	1/8	teaspoon salt
1/3	cup raspberry jam	1/8	teaspoon baking soda
2	eggs	1	cup chopped pecans
1/2	cup packed brown sugar		

Combine 1 1/2 cups flour and sugar in a medium bowl. Cut in the butter with a pastry blender until crumbly. Press the mixture evenly over the bottom of a 9-inch square baking pan.

Bake at 350 degrees for 20 minutes or until the edges are lightly browned. Remove the pan from the oven. Spread the baked layer with the jam.

Combine the eggs and brown sugar in a mixer bowl and mix until well blended. Add 3 tablespoons flour, vanilla, salt and baking soda and mix well. Spread over the jam. Sprinkle with the pecans.

Bake for 22 to 25 minutes or until golden brown.

Cool in the pan on a wire rack. Cut into bars.

Serves 12

Sallie's Chocolate Tarts

A favorite from *Good Cookin' from the Heart of Virginia*

2	eggs	3	tablespoons flour
1/2	cup (1 stick) margarine, melted	3	tablespoons baking cocoa
1	cup sugar	1/3	cup milk
1	cup packed light brown sugar	1	teaspoon vanilla extract
		12	to 14 unbaked tart shells

Beat the eggs lightly in a large bowl. Add the margarine, sugar, brown sugar, flour and baking cocoa and mix well.

Add the milk and vanilla and mix until well blended.

Arrange the tart shells on a baking sheet. Divide the chocolate mixture evenly among the tart shells.

Bake at 350 degrees for 25 minutes or until the filling is set.

Cool the tarts on wire racks.

Garnish with sweetened whipped cream.

Serves 12 to 14

The historic **J.W. Wood Building**, located along Lynchburg's riverfront, is home to central Virginia's children's museum, **Amazement Square**. The modified Greek Revival commercial building was built in the mid-1800s and originally used to store such goods as food, tobacco, and shoes. In 1927, Jessie W. Wood purchased the building where he established his wholesale grocer's business. This business continues today in an adjacent building. Amazement Square began as a Junior League project in 1992. For nearly a decade, committed volunteers from the region worked together to bring to fruition the opening of this hands-on learning center for children.

Amish Apple Pie

4	large McIntosh or Granny Smith apples	1/2	teaspoon cinnamon
1	unbaked (10-inch) pie shell	1	egg
1	cup sugar	1	cup whipping cream
3	tablespoons flour	1	teaspoon vanilla extract
			Streusel

Peel, core and slice the apples. (You should have about 4 cups apple slices.) Place in the pie shell.

Combine the sugar, flour and cinnamon in a medium bowl and mix well. Whisk the egg, whipping cream and vanilla in a small bowl until well blended. Add to the sugar mixture and mix well. Pour over the apples.

Bake at 350 degrees for 20 minutes.

Sprinkle with the Streusel. Bake for 40 minutes longer or until the top is puffed and golden brown.

Serves 10 to 12

Streusel

1/2	cup plus 2 tablespoons flour		Dash of salt
1/3	cup sugar	1/2	cup (1 stick) butter, chilled, sliced
1/4	cup packed brown sugar		
1	teaspoon cinnamon	1/2	cup coarsely chopped English walnuts
1	teaspoon nutmeg		

Place the flour, sugar, brown sugar, cinnamon, nutmeg and salt in a food processor container and process until well mixed. Add the butter 1 slice at a time, processing constantly. Process until the mixture is crumbly. Stir in the walnuts.

Brown Sugar Pies

1/2	cup (1 stick) butter	1/4	cup self-rising flour
1	pound brown sugar	1	teaspoon vanilla extract
4	egg yolks	4	egg whites
3/4	cup milk	2	unbaked (9-inch) pie shells

Melt the butter in a large saucepan over medium heat. Add the brown sugar and mix well.

Whisk the egg yolks in a large bowl. Add the milk, self-rising flour and vanilla and whisk until well blended. Add the brown sugar mixture gradually, stirring constantly.

Beat the egg whites in a mixer bowl at high speed until stiff peaks form.

Fold the stiffly beaten egg whites into the brown sugar mixture gently.

Divide the filling mixture evenly between the pie shells.

Bake at 325 degrees for 50 to 60 minutes or until the fillings are set.

Cool the pies on a wire rack.

May serve with whipped cream or ice cream if desired.

Serves 12 to 16

Clover Hill Village, located approximately one mile from the National Historic Park in Appomattox, is a collection of restored buildings that have been moved from their original locations. Included on the grounds is the 1828 Wesley Chapel, one of the oldest churches in Appomattox County. Although regular worship services haven't been held in the chapel since 1939, it is still used for weddings and special occasions. A log cabin, a blacksmith's shop, and a pole barn containing antique farm equipment and tools are other structures that create this historic glimpse into early American life. Volunteers from the county historical society operate and maintain the village.

World's Fair Ice Cream Pie

1 (4-ounce) package Baker's
   German chocolate
¼ cup (½ stick) margarine or
   butter (optional)
2 to 2½ cups Rice Krispies
   cereal

1 quart coffee ice cream,
   softened
8 ounces light whipped
   topping

Place the chocolate and margarine in a large microwave-safe bowl. Microwave on Medium for 1½ to 2 minutes or until the chocolate is melted.

Stir in the cereal. Press the mixture into a 9- or 10-inch pie plate. Place in the freezer while assembling the filling.

Place the ice cream in a large bowl and stir until smooth and creamy. Fold in the whipped topping. Spoon into the cereal crust.

Freeze for 3 hours. Cover lightly with plastic wrap.

Store, covered, in the freezer for up to 2 days before serving. Leftovers may hold in the freezer for up to a week.

Slicing is easier if the pie is allowed to stand at room temperature for several minutes before serving.

May make your own coffee-flavored ice cream by stirring 1 rounded teaspoonful of instant coffee crystals into 1 quart softened vanilla ice cream.

Serves 6 to 8

Sinful Chocolate Chess Pie

2	eggs	1	teaspoon vanilla extract
1	(5-ounce) can evaporated milk	1½	cups sugar
¼	cup (½ stick) butter, melted	3	tablespoons baking cocoa
		1	unbaked (9-inch) pie shell

Whisk the eggs, evaporated milk, butter and vanilla in a large bowl until well blended. Add the sugar and baking cocoa and mix well. Pour into the pie shell.

Bake at 350 degrees for 30 to 45 minutes or until a knife inserted near the center comes out clean.

Serves 6 to 8

Chocolate Cream Cheese Pie

8	ounces cream cheese, softened	2	egg whites
¼	cup sugar	¼	cup sugar
2	egg yolks, beaten	1	cup whipping cream, whipped
1	teaspoon vanilla extract	1	(9-inch) graham cracker pie shell
6	(1-ounce) semisweet chocolate baking squares, melted		

Beat the cream cheese in a large mixer bowl until light and fluffy. Add ¼ cup sugar, egg yolks and vanilla and mix well. Add the chocolate and mix well.

Beat the egg whites with ¼ cup sugar in a small mixer bowl until stiff peaks form. Fold into the cream cheese mixture gently. Fold in the whipped cream.

Spoon the filling into the crust. Refrigerate, covered, for 5 hours or longer. Garnish with additional whipped cream and shaved chocolate.

Please note that this recipe is prepared using uncooked eggs.

Serves 8

Today, more than 350 events are held annually in the restored **Altavista Train Station**. Norfolk-Southern donated the station to the town of Altavista in 1985. The train station was constructed in 1937 to replace a 1910 structure that burned to the ground. Altavista's original 1908 train station consisted of two railcars: one to house Southern Railroad employees and the second to offer a waiting area for passengers. Rail service to Altavista ended with the 1983 merger between Norfolk & Western and Southern Railroad.

Berry Cobbler

4	cups favorite berries or other fresh fruit
1	teaspoon fresh lemon juice
1/4	to 1/2 cup packed brown sugar
1	cup (scant) flour
1	cup (scant) sugar

1	teaspoon baking powder
1/8	teaspoon salt
1	egg
1/4	teaspoon almond extract
6	tablespoons melted butter
1/4	cup sugar

Place the berries in a 2-quart baking dish. Sprinkle with the lemon juice and enough brown sugar to sweeten as desired and toss lightly.

Combine the flour, 1 cup sugar, baking powder and salt in a bowl and mix well.

Whisk the egg and almond extract in a bowl until well blended. Add to the flour mixture and mix lightly with a fork until the mixture clings together.

Knead the dough with your fingers until well mixed. Crumble over the berry mixture.

Drizzle with the melted butter and sprinkle with 1/4 cup sugar.

Bake at 350 degrees for 40 minutes. Serve warm.

May use your favorite berries or other fruit in season but be sure to sample for sweetness and adjust the sugar amounts to taste.

Serves 8

Quick and Easy Chocolate Mousse

1 1/2 cups whipping cream
2 cups semisweet chocolate chips
1 1/2 teaspoons vanilla extract
Pinch of salt

6 egg yolks, beaten
2 egg whites
1 cup whipping cream

Heat the 1 1/2 cups whipping cream just to the simmering point.

Place the chocolate chips, vanilla and salt in a blender container and process for 30 seconds. Pour in hot cream gradually, processing constantly. Process for 30 seconds longer or until the chocolate is completely melted and the mixture is well blended.

Add the egg yolks and process for 5 seconds or just until blended. Pour the mixture into a large bowl. Let stand until cool.

Beat the egg whites in a mixer bowl until stiff peaks form. Fold the stiffly beaten egg whites into the chocolate mixture gently.

Spoon into a serving bowl or wine glasses. Refrigerate, covered with plastic wrap, until chilled.

Whip the 1 cup whipping cream in a mixer bowl until soft peaks form. Top the mousse with the whipped cream.

Serves 6

Eclair Dessert

1	cup water	3	(4-ounce) packages vanilla instant pudding mix
1/2	cup (1 stick) butter		
1	cup flour	4	cups milk
3	eggs	8	ounces whipped topping
8	ounces cream cheese, softened		Chocolate syrup (optional)
			Berries (optional)

Place the water and butter in a medium saucepan. Bring to a boil over high heat. Remove the saucepan from the heat. Add the flour all at once and stir vigorously with a wooden spoon until the dough pulls away from the side of the pan and forms a ball.

Add the eggs 1 at a time, beating with the spoon after each addition until well blended.

Spread the dough over the bottom and up the sides of a 9x13-inch baking pan.

Bake at 400 degrees for 35 minutes or until golden brown.

Let stand in the pan on a wire rack until cooled completely.

Combine the cream cheese and pudding mixes in a bowl and beat until well blended. Add the milk gradually, mixing well after each addition.

Spread the cream cheese mixture over the cooled crust. Cover with the whipped topping. Drizzle with the chocolate syrup and top with berries.

Chill, loosely covered, until serving time.

Serves 15

Spanish Coffee

A favorite from *Good Cookin' from the Heart of Virginia*

1	**jigger Tia Maria**	2	**tablespoons sweetened**
1/2	**jigger brandy**		**whipped cream**
1	**cup hot brewed coffee**		

Stir the Tia Maria and brandy into the coffee. Top with the whipped cream.

Serves 1

Crunchy Topping for Ice Cream

1/2	**cup (1 stick) butter**	1/2	**cup chopped pecans and/or**
1	**cup packed brown sugar**		**almonds**
2 1/2	**cups cornflakes**		

Place the butter and brown sugar in a saucepan. Bring to a boil over medium-high heat. Reduce the heat to medium-low. Simmer for 2 minutes.

Combine the cornflakes and pecans in a large bowl. Add the butter mixture and toss lightly. Spread on a nonstick baking sheet to cool completely. Break into pieces and store in a tightly covered container.

Serve over any favorite ice cream.

Serves 8 to 12

*Now privately owned, the Federal style **Sandusky House**, built in 1808, served as Civil War headquarters to General David Hunter during the June 1864 Battle of Lynchburg. Major George C. Hutter, a former Army paymaster and pre-war associate of General Hunter's, owned the house. Hunter's staff included two future U.S. Presidents, Colonel Rutherford B. Hayes and Captain William McKinley. An adjacent brick barn, now demolished, served as a Union hospital during the fighting. General Hunter's abrupt retreat, which concluded the two-day Battle of Lynchburg, left 117 seriously wounded Union soldiers abandoned on this site.*

Chocolate Trifle

1	(2-layer) package chocolate cake mix	⅓	cup coffee liqueur
3	(4-ounce) packages instant chocolate pudding mix	16	ounces whipped topping
6	cups milk	6	to 8 toffee candy bars, broken into small pieces

Prepare and bake the cake mix according to the package directions for 2 round cake pans.

Cool the layers in the pans for 10 minutes. Remove the layers from the pans and cool completely on wire racks.

Combine the pudding mix and milk in a large bowl and mix with a wire whisk until well blended. Refrigerate, covered, until ready to use.

Place 1 of the cake layers in a large trifle bowl or other glass bowl. Poke holes in the cake layer with the end of a wooden spoon. Drizzle with half the liqueur.

Add layers of half the pudding, half the whipped topping and half the crushed candy.

Place the second cake layer in the bowl and repeat the layers of pudding, whipped topping and candy.

Refrigerate, covered, until ready to serve.

Serves 16

Punch Bowl Cake

1 (2-layer) package yellow cake mix
2 (4-ounce) packages vanilla or chocolate instant pudding mix
4 cups milk
1 (21-ounce) can cherry pie filling
1 (16-ounce) can crushed pineapple, drained
2 bananas, sliced
16 ounces whipped topping
Flaked coconut
Chopped pecans
Chopped maraschino cherries

Prepare and bake the cake mix according to the package directions.

Prepare the pudding mix according to the package directions, using 4 cups milk.

Crumble the cooled cake into bite-size pieces.

Place half the cake pieces in a punch bowl or trifle bowl. Layer the pie filling, pudding, pineapple, bananas and whipped topping 1/2 at a time in the bowl. Repeat the layers.

Top the trifle with a sprinkle of flaked coconut, chopped pecans and/or chopped cherries.

Refrigerate, covered, until ready to serve.

May substitute an angel food cake torn into bite-size pieces for the yellow cake.

Serves 16

The restoration of Lynchburg's **Academy of Music** is anticipated by 2002, nearly a century after its original opening in 1905. The Academy hosted live theatre and music performances, as well as "moving pictures" from its opening until 1958. Academy performers included such greats as George M. Cohan, Sarah Bernhardt, Gene Autry, pianist Paderewski, Eubie Blake, and John Philip Sousa. Other notable appearances include performances by the Three Stooges, Russian ballerina Pavlova, Houdini, and the Ziegfeld Follies. When a fire destroyed the original building in 1911, department store magnate C.M. Guggenheimer spearheaded the rebuilding. Although movies were the mainstay of the Academy after 1928, live performances continued in the structure, which is recognized for its outstanding acoustics. The renovated and revitalized Academy will host touring headliners and local performing arts groups.

Pumpkin Dump Cake

3   *eggs, lightly beaten*
1   *(29-ounce) can pumpkin*
1   *cup sugar*
1   *tablespoon cinnamon*
3/4   *teaspoon salt*
1   *(12-ounce) can evaporated
      milk*

1   *(2-layer) package yellow
      cake mix*
1/2   *cup chopped pecans*
3/4   *cup (1 1/2 sticks) butter,
      melted*

Combine the eggs, pumpkin, sugar, cinnamon and salt in a large bowl and mix well.

Add the evaporated milk gradually, stirring until well blended. Pour into a greased 9x13-inch baking pan.

Sprinkle the dry cake mix evenly over the pumpkin mixture. Sprinkle with the pecans. Drizzle the butter over the top.

Bake at 350 degrees for 50 to 60 minutes or until the pumpkin mixture is set and the topping is golden brown.

Cool in the pan on a wire rack.

Serve topped with dollops of whipped topping or scoops of vanilla ice cream.

Serves 15

Door to Door

Chicken Noodle Soup

1	cup chopped carrot	1/4	teaspoon salt
1	cup chopped parsnips	1/4	teaspoon pepper
1/2	cup thinly sliced celery	2	cups wide egg noodles
1	tablespoon margarine or butter	1	pound boneless skinless chicken breasts, cut into
1	tablespoon flour		1-inch pieces
3 1/2	cups reduced-sodium chicken broth	2	tablespoons chopped fresh parsley
1	cup water		Melba Toast

Sauté the carrot, parsnips and celery in the margarine in a large Dutch oven over medium-high heat for 3 minutes.

Stir in the flour. Add the broth and water gradually, whisking constantly. Season with the salt and pepper. Bring to a boil.

Simmer, covered, over low heat for 5 minutes, stirring occasionally. Add the noodles and chicken. Bring to a boil over medium heat.

Simmer, covered, over low heat for 10 minutes, stirring occasionally. Stir in the parsley. Ladle into soup bowls. Serve with Melba Toast.

Serves 8

Melba Toast

1	loaf thinly sliced bread	1	cup (2 sticks) butter, melted

Preheat the oven to 500 degrees. Cut the bread into halves. Arrange on a baking sheet. Brush with the butter. Place in the oven. Turn the oven off. Let stand in the oven for 8 to 10 hours.

May cook in a 250-degree oven for 1 hour. Drain on paper towels until most of the butter is absorbed. Store, tightly covered, at room temperature.

Photograph on overleaf:
**Murrell House—
Garland Hill**
by Robert DeVaul

French Market Soup

A favorite from *Good Cookin' from the Heart of Virginia*

4	sprigs of fresh parsley	2	garlic cloves, minced
1/2	teaspoon thyme		Salt and pepper to taste
1	bay leaf	1	pound smoked sausage or
2	cups dried bean soup mix		kielbasa
1	smoked ham hock	2	boneless skinless chicken
3	quarts water		breasts
1	(28-ounce) can tomatoes	1/2	cup red wine
2	onions, chopped	1/2	cup chopped fresh parsley
4	ribs of celery, chopped		

Tie the parsley, thyme and bay leaf in a piece of cheesecloth to make a bouquet garni. Sort and rinse the beans.

Combine the beans, ham hock, water and bouquet garni in a stockpot and mix well. Simmer, covered, over low heat for 2 1/2 to 3 hours, stirring occasionally.

Add the undrained tomatoes, onions, celery, garlic, salt and pepper and mix well. Simmer, covered, for 1 1/2 hours, stirring occasionally.

Slice the sausage as desired. Cut the chicken into the desired-size pieces. Stir the sausage and chicken into the soup.

Simmer, covered, for 30 to 40 minutes.

Add the wine and parsley and mix well. Discard the bouquet garni. Ladle the soup into soup bowls.

Serves 10

Door-to-Door Meals, or Friendship Meals, are a popular way to convey caring to a family or friend. What better way to welcome a new mother and baby home from the hospital than to prepare a meal for the entire family? Friendship Meals can say thank you to the neighbor who looks after your pets while you're on vacation. These dishes, accompanied by a salad, dessert, and a bottle of wine, are a thoughtful way to thank your hosts following a trip to their beach house or ski bungalow. Friendship Meals can also express appreciation to the piano teacher, soccer coach, carpool mom, or any number of people who go the extra mile for you and your family. A home-cooked meal delivered to a doorstep welcomes a newcomer or offers congratulations or condolences.

Deluxe Beef Stew

2 **pounds lean beef**	1 **(10-ounce) can beef bouillon**
¼ **cup (½ stick) butter**	2 **tablespoons chopped fresh**
8 **ounces onion, chopped**	**parsley**
8 **ounces mushrooms, chopped**	1½ **cups dry red wine**
1 **tablespoon flour**	

Cut the beef into 1-inch pieces.

Brown the beef on all sides in half the butter in a skillet. Remove the beef to a plate.

Add the remaining butter to the skillet. Sauté the onion and mushrooms in the butter until the onion is tender.

Remove the onion mixture with a slotted spoon to a plate, reserving the pan drippings.

Add the flour to the reserved pan drippings. Cook over low heat for 5 minutes or until the mixture is smooth, stirring constantly.

Stir in the bouillon, parsley and red wine. Add the beef, onion and mushrooms and mix well.

Simmer, covered, over low heat for 2 to 3 hours. Serve the stew in a bread bowl or over egg noodles or rice.

May add potatoes, carrots or other vegetables before simmering.

Serves 6

Brunswick Stew

A favorite from Good Cookin' from the Heart of Virginia

1	(2½- to 3-pound) chicken	2	(10-ounce) packages frozen baby lima beans
4	cups water		
4	potatoes, peeled, chopped	1	tablespoon sugar
4	onions, sliced	1	tablespoon salt
2	(16-ounce) cans white corn, drained	½	teaspoon black pepper Cayenne to taste
1	(28-ounce) can tomatoes	1½	teaspoons celery seeds
1	(6-ounce) can tomato paste		

Cook the chicken in the water in a stockpot over medium heat for 1 hour or until tender.

Remove the chicken to a cutting board. Let stand until cool. Reserve 2 cups of the broth.

Bone and chop the chicken. Discard the skin and bones.

Boil the potatoes and onions in water to cover in a saucepan for 20 minutes; drain.

Combine the reserved broth, chicken, corn, tomatoes, tomato paste, lima beans, sugar, salt, black pepper, cayenne and celery seeds in a stockpot and mix well. Stir in the potato mixture.

Simmer, covered, over low heat for 45 minutes.

Serves 12 to 16

French Bread Lasagna

1	pound ground beef	³/₄	teaspoon salt
¹/₃	cup chopped onion	¹/₂	teaspoon pepper
¹/₃	cup chopped celery	4	large tomatoes, sliced
2	garlic cloves, minced		¹/₂ inch thick
14	(¹/₂-inch-thick) slices French	2	teaspoons olive oil
	bread, toasted	3	tablespoons butter
1	teaspoon basil	3	tablespoons flour
1	teaspoon parsley flakes	1¹/₂	cups milk
1	teaspoon oregano	¹/₃	cup grated Parmesan cheese
1	teaspoon rosemary	2	cups shredded mozzarella
1	teaspoon garlic powder		cheese

Brown the ground beef with the onion, celery and garlic in a skillet, stirring until the ground beef is crumbly; drain.

Line the bottom of a 9x13-inch baking dish with 10 slices of the bread. Crumble the remaining bread.

Combine the basil, parsley, oregano, rosemary, garlic powder, salt and pepper in a bowl and mix well.

Layer half the ground beef mixture, half the tomatoes and half the seasoning mixture over the bread. Drizzle with half the olive oil. Sprinkle with the remaining crumbled bread. Layer with the remaining ground beef mixture, tomatoes, seasoning mixture and olive oil.

Melt the butter in a saucepan over medium heat. Add the flour, stirring until smooth. Stir in the milk gradually, stirring constantly. Bring to a boil. Cook for 2 minutes or until thick and bubbly, stirring constantly.

Remove from the heat. Add the Parmesan cheese and mix well. Pour over the layers. Top with the mozzarella cheese. Bake at 350 degrees for 40 to 45 minutes.

Serves 8 to 10

Baked Pizza Pasta

1	pound bow tie pasta
1	(28-ounce) can Italian tomatoes
¼	cup (½ stick) butter
¼	cup flour
1½	cups milk
	Salt and pepper to taste
1½	cups shredded mozzarella cheese
1	cup chopped fontina cheese
1⅓	cups grated Romano cheese
½	cup finely chopped fresh parsley

Cook the bow tie pasta al dente, according to package directions. Keep warm.

Drain the tomatoes, reserving 1¼ cups of the liquid. Chop the tomatoes.

Melt the butter in a heavy saucepan over medium-low heat. Add the flour. Cook for 3 minutes, whisking constantly.

Add the milk and reserved tomato liquid, whisking constantly. Bring to a boil, whisking frequently.

Stir in the tomatoes, salt and pepper. Simmer for 3 minutes or until thickened, stirring frequently.

Combine the sauce with the pasta, mozzarella cheese, fontina cheese, 1 cup of the Romano cheese and parsley in a large bowl and toss to mix well. Spoon into a buttered shallow 3- to 4-quart baking dish.

Sprinkle with the remaining ⅓ cup Romano cheese. Bake at 375 degrees for 30 to 35 minutes or until golden brown and bubbly.

Serves 6 to 8

Lynchburg Baptist Seminary was founded in 1886 and construction of the first building began in 1888. The seminary's first commencement occurred on January 13, 1890 with a class of 33 students. Harlem-Renaissance writer Anne Bethel Spencer was valedictorian of the class of 1899. Lynchburg Baptist Seminary later became the Virginia Seminary, and the institution's name changed several more times before its current name, **Virginia University of Lynchburg***, was adopted in 1996. As a fundraising strategy, the president of the institution, Elisha G. Hall, hopes to reach a total of 200,000 donors who will each contribute $1 to the school's capital campaign. Students can attain either a two-year or a four-year degree.*

Budget Shepherd's Pie

2	pounds (about) ground beef	1	tablespoon (or less) MSG
2	large onions, chopped	10	cups well-seasoned mashed
5	eggs, beaten		potatoes
2	teaspoons garlic salt	2	tablespoons melted butter
1	teaspoon pepper		

Cook the ground beef in a large skillet until brown and crumbly, stirring frequently. Drain the ground beef well and measure 4 cups of the cooked ground beef for the recipe. Reserve any remaining cooked ground beef for another purpose.

Combine the ground beef, onions, eggs, garlic salt, pepper and MSG in a bowl and mix well.

Spread half the potatoes evenly over the bottom of a buttered 9x13-inch baking dish. Add layers of the ground beef mixture and the remaining potatoes.

Brush the top of the potatoes with the melted butter. Bake at 400 degrees for 1 hour or until the top is puffy and golden brown.

Let the Shepherd's Pie rest for several minutes if you wish to serve by cutting into squares.

Serves 8

Rosy Red Chicken

¾	cup rosé	1	teaspoon ginger powder
¼	cup soy sauce	¼	teaspoon oregano
¼	cup vegetable oil	¼	teaspoon garlic powder
2	tablespoons water	4	to 6 boneless skinless
1	tablespoon brown sugar		chicken breasts

Combine the rosé, soy sauce, oil, water, brown sugar, ginger, oregano and garlic powder in a bowl and mix well. Pour into a deep baking dish.

Add the chicken, turning to coat. Bake, covered, at 350 degrees for 1 hour or until the chicken is cooked through.

Serves 4 to 6

Picante Chicken

4 boneless skinless chicken breasts
1 envelope taco seasoning mix
½ cup flour
½ cup (1 stick) margarine, melted
1 (10-ounce) package tortilla chips, crushed
8 ounces shredded four-cheese Mexican blend
1 (24-ounce) jar picante sauce

Coat the chicken with a mixture of the taco seasoning mix and flour. Dip in the margarine in a shallow bowl. Coat with the tortilla chips.

Arrange in a baking dish sprayed with nonstick cooking spray. Bake at 375 degrees for 35 minutes or until cooked through.

Sprinkle with the cheese. Pour the picante sauce over the top. Bake for 10 minutes longer. Serve with Spanish rice.

Serves 4

Trapshooting, hunting, and horseback riding were the primary activities for members of the Oakwood Gun Club. The name **Oakwood Country Club** was adopted in 1902 when the gun club added a bowling alley, tennis courts, and a clubhouse. Originally located near Riverside Park in Lynchburg, the Club planned to add a golf course in 1914. This addition necessitated a move to 100 acres on what was formerly the Clopton farm. Architect Minor Lewis designed the clubhouse, which is recognized as one of Virginia's largest bungalow-style structures.

Corn and Shrimp Casserole

2	cups chopped cooked shrimp	1/2	teaspoon dry mustard
2	tablespoons chopped onion	3	eggs
3	tablespoons chopped green bell pepper	1	(8-ounce) can cream-style corn
1/4	cup butter	1	cup milk
3	tablespoons flour		

Sauté the shrimp, onion and green pepper in the butter in a skillet until the onion and green pepper are tender.

Combine the flour and dry mustard in a large bowl and mix well. Beat the eggs in a small bowl. Mix in the corn and milk. Add the corn mixture to the flour mixture and mix well.

Add the sautéed shrimp mixture and stir until well mixed. Spoon into a greased baking dish.

Bake at 350 degrees for 40 minutes or until set and golden brown.

Serve with turkey or ham.

Serves 6

Hot Chicken Salad

6	cups chopped cooked chicken breasts	1 1/2	cups mayonnaise
1	(8-ounce) can sliced water chestnuts, drained	1	teaspoon lemon juice
1/2	cup chopped onion		Salt and pepper to taste
1/2	cup sliced celery	2	cups shredded Cheddar cheese
			Crushed potato chips to taste

Combine the chicken and water chestnuts in a large bowl. Add the onion and celery and toss lightly to mix.

Blend the mayonnaise and lemon juice in a small bowl and mix in salt and pepper.

Add the mayonnaise mixture to the chicken mixture and toss lightly until well mixed. Spoon into a lightly greased baking dish.

Sprinkle the Cheddar cheese and crushed potato chips evenly over the top.

Bake at 350 degrees for 45 minutes or until hot and bubbly.

Serves 6 to 8

The **Old Court House**, designed in the Greek Revival style by Virginia and Tennessee Railroad architect and civil engineer, William S. Ellison, was built in 1855. The existing building, current home of the Lynchburg Museum System, replaced an 1813 courthouse known as Lynchburg's "chief disgrace" because of its appearance. In 1851, one year before Lynchburg became incorporated as a city, the town's citizens voted to erect a new courthouse. The court-house's old town clock was made in Boston in 1835 and was first installed on the original St. Paul's Episcopal church building, then located at Seventh and Church Streets. The clock was removed in 1850, repaired, and incorporated into Ellison's Court House plan.

Tomato and Vidalia Onion Tart

2	large Vidalia onions	8	ounces Gruyère cheese,
2	tablespoons butter		shredded
2	or 3 large tomatoes	3	or 4 fresh basil leaves,
1	(9-inch) pie shell		chopped
	Salt and pepper to taste		

Cut the onions into thin slices.

Sauté the onions in the butter in a skillet for 15 minutes or until tender and translucent. Remove the onions to a plate to cool.

Slice the tomatoes carefully. Drain the tomato slices on paper towels.

Spread the sautéed onions evenly over the bottom of the pie shell. Sprinkle with salt, pepper and ³⁄₄ of the Gruyère cheese.

Arrange the tomato slices over the onions, overlapping as needed. Sprinkle with the basil, salt and pepper. Top with the remaining Gruyère cheese.

Bake at 375 degrees for 40 minutes or until the pie shell is golden brown.

Let stand for 5 minutes before cutting into wedges.

This is great with any grilled beef, pork or chicken.

Serves 6

Pumpkin Spice Cake

1	(2-layer) package yellow cake mix	1	(4-ounce) package French vanilla pudding and pie filling mix
1	teaspoon nutmeg		
1	teaspoon ground cloves	½	cup vegetable oil
1	teaspoon allspice	½	cup water
1	teaspoon cinnamon	3	eggs
1	teaspoon salt		Confectioners' sugar to taste
¾	cup mashed cooked pumpkin		

Sift the cake mix, nutmeg, cloves, allspice, cinnamon and salt together into a large mixer bowl.

Add the pumpkin, pudding and pie filling mix, oil, water and eggs. Beat for 2 minutes or until smooth.

Spoon the batter into a greased bundt pan.

Bake at 375 degrees for 45 to 50 minutes or until the cake tests done.

Cool in the pan on a wire rack for 10 minutes.

Invert the cake onto a serving plate. Top with a sprinkle of confectioners' sugar.

Serves 16

Sweet Briar College was founded in 1901, the bequest of Indiana Fletcher Williams in memory of her daughter, Daisy, who died at age 16. The Italianate plantation house is now the home of the college's president. Twenty-two Sweet Briar buildings, designed in the neo-Georgian style by the noted architect Ralph Adams Cram, comprise the Sweet Briar College National Historic District. Located on 3,300 acres north of Lynchburg, Sweet Briar is a top-ranked private liberal arts and sciences college for women and is affiliated with the Virginia Center for the Creative Arts. Sweet Briar's art gallery, museum, and cultural activities are open to the general public, most free of charge. The Florence Elston Inn is open year-round to area visitors. A walking tour is available.

Heavenly Brownies

1	cup (2 sticks) butter	1	tablespoon vanilla extract
2	cups sugar	1½	cups self-rising flour
½	cup baking cocoa	1	cup chopped pecans
4	eggs		

Melt the butter in a saucepan over low heat or microwave in a microwave-safe bowl on Medium just until melted.

Combine the butter, sugar and baking cocoa in a bowl and mix until smooth and well-blended.

Add the eggs and vanilla and blend well.

Stir in the self-rising flour just until moistened.

Fold in the pecans.

Spread the batter evenly in a greased and floured 9x13-inch baking pan.

Bake at 350 degrees for 30 minutes or just until the brownies pull from the side of the pan.

Cool in the pan on a wire rack. Cut into bars.

Serves 15

City Fare

Quesadillas

2 (12-inch) flour tortillas	1 cup chopped cooked shrimp,
³/₄ cup shredded Cheddar cheese	beef or chicken
³/₄ cup shredded mozzarella	Sour cream
cheese	Salsa
2 tablespoons chopped	Jalapeños
scallions	

Spray a large skillet with nonstick cooking spray or grease lightly. Preheat the skillet over medium heat.

Place one tortilla in the hot skillet. Sprinkle with the Cheddar cheese, mozzarella cheese, scallions and shrimp. Top with the remaining tortilla.

Heat until the cheese melts. Turn the quesadilla over. Heat until golden brown.

Place the quesadilla on a serving plate. Cut into triangles. Serve with the sour cream, salsa and jalapeños.

Serves 2   Abe McWane and Steve Hooten, Boodles

Marinated Goat Cheese

4 logs goat cheese	1¹/₂ tablespoons dried thyme
1¹/₂ cups extra-virgin olive oil	3 large garlic cloves, cut into
4 bay leaves	slivers
1¹/₂ tablespoons mixed	3 tablespoons minced fresh
peppercorns	basil

Cut each cheese log into 5 slices. Arrange the slices in a large heat-proof dish; do not allow the slices to touch each other.

Combine the olive oil, bay leaves, peppercorns and thyme in a small saucepan. Heat until the mixture begins to sizzle and pop. Pour over the cheese. Sprinkle with the garlic and basil.

Marinate, covered, in the refrigerator overnight.

Let stand until the cheese comes to room temperature. Serve with French bread.

Serves 8 to 10   Lucy Cook, Magnolia Foods

Photograph on overleaf:
Monument Terrace
courtesy of the
City of Lynchburg

French Mushroom Soup

$1/2$	cup chopped onion	$1/4$	cup margarine
$1/4$	cup margarine	3	pounds fresh mushrooms, sliced
6	tablespoons flour		
12	cups chicken broth	$1/2$	teaspoon salt
$1^1/2$	tablespoons dried parsley flakes	1	teaspoon fresh lemon juice
		2	cups whipping cream
$1/2$	bay leaf		Sherry to taste
$1/8$	teaspoon dried thyme		

Sauté the onion in $1/4$ cup margarine in a large soup pot until tender. Sprinkle with the flour and cook over low heat for 4 minutes, stirring constantly; do not brown.

Stir in the broth gradually. Cook until thickened, stirring constantly. Add the parsley, bay leaf and thyme. Simmer for 20 minutes, stirring frequently.

Melt $1/4$ cup margarine in a large skillet. Add the mushrooms, salt and lemon juice and toss until well mixed. Cook for 5 minutes, tossing frequently.

Add the mushroom mixture to the broth mixture and mix gently. Simmer for 5 minutes, stirring frequently. (If soup is not to be served immediately, remove from the heat and set aside to reheat later.)

Stir the whipping cream and sherry into the simmering soup. Heat to just below the simmering point, stirring frequently.

Adjust the seasonings. Discard the bay leaf. Ladle into soup bowls and garnish with chopped fresh parsley. Serve immediately.

May substitute $1^1/2$ pounds of shiitake mushrooms for half of the mushrooms. May thicken if desired to serve as a sauce for pasta.

Serves 12   *Rie and Eddie Godsey, Meriwether's Market Restaurant*

Lynchburg's **Monument Terrace** commemorates area soldiers who lost their lives in combat. Monument Terrace was designed by Aubrey Chesterman and was originally conceived as a memorial to the Lynchburg soldiers who died during World War I. Often likened to Rome's famed Spanish Steps, the terrace is constructed of granite and limestone in a style reminiscent of the Italian Renaissance and Baroque periods. The decorative stairway is flanked by azaleas and features monuments on several levels, commemorating those who died in other wars and conflicts. Built to connect Church and Court Streets, Monument Terrace also marks the entrance to the Old Court House. A trademark of the City of Lynchburg, Monument Terrace features 137 steps.

Shrimp Bisque

$1/3$ to $1/2$ cup chopped onion	2 tablespoons tomato paste
$1/3$ to $1/2$ cup chopped carrot	$1/4$ cup brandy
2 tablespoons butter	$3/4$ cup white wine
1 pound (26- to 30-count) peeled shrimp, or $1/2$ pounds crab meat or bay scallops	4 cups Velouté Soup Base
	2 cups fish or chicken stock
	1 cup heavy cream
1 bay leaf	Salt and white pepper
Pinch of thyme	to taste
4 parsley stems	

Sauté the onion and carrot in the butter in a 3-quart saucepan until light golden color. Cut the shrimp into desired size pieces and add to saucepan. Add the bay leaf, thyme and parsley and sauté until the shrimp turn pink.

Add the tomato paste and mix well. Stir in the brandy, wine, Velouté Soup Base and stock. Simmer for 10 minutes, stirring frequently. Discard the bay leaf. Process the mixture in a food processor or blender in several batches, pulsing until the mixture is of the desired consistency. Return to the saucepan.

Stir in the cream, season with salt and white pepper and heat to serving temperature. Ladle the bisque into soup bowls and garnish with chopped fresh chives.

Serves 10   *Ken Huggins, Winton Country Club*

Velouté Soup Base

$1/2$ cup minced onion or leek	3 to 4 cups chicken or fish stock, milk or vegetable liquid
2 tablespoons butter	Salt and pepper to taste
2 tablespoons flour	

Cook the onion in butter in a covered saucepan over medium-low heat for 7 to 8 minutes or until tender. Stir in the flour gradually. Cook for about 3 minutes, stirring constantly; do not brown. Heat 1 cup of the stock. Remove the flour mixture from the heat. Allow the mixture to stand for a few seconds until the bubbling stops. Whisk in the hot stock and 2 cups of the remaining stock.

Simmer for 10 minutes or until the mixture coats a spoon, stirring frequently. Add spoonfuls of the remaining stock until of the desired consistency. Season with salt and pepper.

Makes 3 to 4 cups

Sweet Red Pepper Soup

6   fresh red bell peppers
4   cups heavy cream

6   ounces lump crab meat
     Sea salt to taste

Seed and chop the red peppers.

Combine the red peppers and cream in a soup pot. Simmer for 6 to 7 minutes or until the red peppers are soft.

Purée the mixture in a food processor, strain and return to the soup pot.

Bring the soup to a simmer.

Discard any shell from the crab meat. Add the crab meat to the soup.

Season the soup with sea salt, adding additional sea salt if the soup seems bitter.

Ladle into soup bowls and garnish with chopped fresh chives.

May substitute store-bought roasted red peppers for the fresh red bell peppers.

Serves 6　　　　　　　*Rie and Eddie Godsey, Meriwether's Market Restaurant*

A tradition for over 200 years, Lynchburg's **Community Market** *was established in 1783, several blocks from its present location between Main and Church Streets. The market was first a fresh-air marketplace for area craftsmen, bakers, and farmers. A Market Comr ttee, established in 1839, upgraded the original marketplace, which existed until 1909 at a nearby Main Street location. Renowned architect, Stanhope Johnson, designed the existing armory and adjacent Community Marketplace in 1932. Renovations have maintained the condition and appeal of the Community Market, and it is widely used as a marketplace for crafts, baked goods, and produce, as well as a central location for community events and downtown gatherings.*

Gazpacho

1/3	French baguette, or 3 slices white bread		1	red bell pepper, seeded
3	tablespoons fresh lemon juice		20	to 30 ounces V-8 vegetable juice cocktail
3	garlic cloves		3	tablespoons balsamic vinegar
6	large ripe tomatoes, seeded		3	tablespoons fruity olive oil
1	bunch scallions			Salt and pepper to taste
3	cucumbers, seeded			Tabasco sauce to taste
1	yellow bell pepper, seeded			

Combine the bread, lemon juice and garlic in a food processor container and process until smooth. Pour into a large bowl.

Cut the tomatoes, scallions, cucumbers and bell peppers into large chunks. Process the vegetables in batches in the food processor by pulsing until chopped as desired.

Stir the vegetable mixture into the bread mixture.

Add enough of the V-8 juice to make the gazpacho of the desired consistency.

Whisk in the vinegar, olive oil, salt, pepper and Tabasco sauce. Refrigerate, covered, for 4 hours or longer.

Serves 6   *Lucy Cook, Magnolia Foods*

Strawberry, Walnut and Roquefort Salad

Mesclun
Romaine
Leaf lettuce
Sliced grilled chicken (optional)
Green bell pepper
Cucumber

Red onion
Toasted walnuts
Roquefort cheese, crumbled
Strawberries, quartered
Croutons
Creamy Raspberry Vinaigrette

Combine the mesclun, roamine and leaf lettuce in a large salad bowl and toss lightly to mix. Place a layer of the greens in salad bowls or on salad plates.

Chop the green pepper, cucumber and red onion into bite-size pieces. Arrange the desired amount of vegetables and chicken on the greens. Sprinkle with the walnuts, cheese, strawberries and croutons.

Drizzle the desired amount of the Creamy Raspberry Vinaigrette over the salad and serve immediately.

May substitute other vegetables for the green bell pepper, cucumber and red onion.

Serves a variable number   Joan Virginia Lingerfelt, The Briar Patch

Creamy Raspberry Vinaigrette

$^1/_2$ cup chopped onion
$^1/_2$ cup sugar
$^1/_4$ cup raspberry vinegar
1   teaspoon celery seeds

1   teaspoon dry mustard
1   teaspoon salt
     Red food coloring (optional)
1   cup vegetable oil

Combine the onion, sugar, vinegar, celery seeds, dry mustard, salt and food coloring in a blender container. Process for 2 minutes.

Add the oil a few drops at a time, processing constantly. Process the mixture for 2 minutes longer.

Store in the refrigerator. May add a small amount of water to thin the vinaigrette to the desired consistency.

Makes 2$^1/_4$ cups

Vintner's Salad

1/2	cup walnuts	1	red apple
1	tablespoon margarine	1	pear
	Salt to taste	2	tablespoons (about) orange juice
2	pounds mixed greens (choose 2 or 3 from the following: spinach, radicchio, leaf lettuce, Belgian endive, romaine, arugula)	1 1/4	cups Bleu Cheese Vinaigrette

Arrange the walnuts on a baking sheet. Dot with the margarine and sprinkle with salt. Bake at 350 degrees for 8 minutes. Stir occasionally to coat evenly with the margarine. Spread the toasted walnuts on a paper towel to cool.

Rinse the greens and pat dry. Tear the greens gently into bite-size pieces and place in a large salad bowl.

Core the unpeeled apple and pear and cut into thin slices or small chunks. Toss the fruit in orange juice to prevent discoloration; drain.

Add the fruit and Bleu Cheese Vinaigrette to the greens, tossing to mix. Top with the toasted walnuts.

May toss the greens with the Bleu Cheese Vinaigrette, arrange the fruit over the greens and top with the toasted walnuts. May substitute other fruits for the apple and pear for a variety of tastes and colors.

Serves 10   *Rie and Eddie Godsey, Meriwether's Market Restaurant*

Bleu Cheese Vinaigrette

6	tablespoons red wine vinegar	1	tablespoon pepper
1/4	cup fresh lemon juice	1/2	cup olive oil or walnut oil
2	tablespoons Dijon mustard	2/3	cup vegetable oil
2	teaspoons salt	4	ounces bleu cheese, crumbled

Blend the vinegar, lemon juice, Dijon mustard, salt and pepper in a bowl.

Add the oils gradually, beating constantly with a wire whisk or electric mixer until the mixture is slightly thickened and well mixed. Stir in the bleu cheese.

Makes 2 cups

Summer Chicken Salad

6	boneless skinless chicken breasts		2	tablespoons chopped celery
1/2	cup chopped grapes		2	tablespoons chopped onion
2	tablespoons sliced almonds		1/2	cup mayonnaise

Bake the chicken at 350 degrees for 45 minutes or until tender. Let stand until cool, chop into small pieces and place in a bowl.

Add the grapes, almonds, celery and onion and toss to mix. Add the mayonnaise and mix well.

Serve on a bed of lettuce as a salad. May use as the filling for a sandwich.

Serves 7 to 8   *Eric Spain, Percival's Isle Java Tavern*

Smoked Whitefish Salad

1	pound smoked whitefish		2	sprigs of fresh dill, chopped
1	cup finely chopped celery			Salt and freshly ground
	Juice of 1/2 lemon			pepper to taste
1	to 1 1/2 cups mayonnaise			

Skin and bone the whitefish. Place in a bowl and flake.

Add the celery, lemon juice, mayonnaise, dill, salt and pepper and mix well. Adjust the seasonings if necessary.

Serve on a bed of lettuce as a main dish salad. May also serve as an appetizer.

Serves 2   *Urs and Michelle Gabathuler, Main Street Eatery and Catering Company*

Avenel, built in 1838 by William and Frances Burwell, was a nineteenth-century centerpiece of Bedford's social, cultural, and political life. The home's unique architectural features, such as the extensive wraparound porch, earned Avenel a spot on both the National Register of Historic Places and the Virginia Landmark Register. The Bedford home has hosted many distinguished visitors, including Edgar Allen Poe and Robert E. Lee. Lee brought his wife to Avenel to benefit from the clean mountain air. Today, the historic home is being restored to its original grandeur by the Avenel Foundation. It is currently used for business and social gatherings. Avenel's benevolent ghost, "The White Lady," is said to inhabit the premises.

Steamed Asparagus with Tomato Vinaigrette

2	pounds fresh asparagus spears		Tomato Vinaigrette
		1/3	cup grated Parmesan cheese

Discard tough ends from the asparagus. Steam or blanch for 3 to 5 minutes or just until the asparagus is tender-crisp. Drain well and place on a serving platter.

Drizzle the Tomato Vinaigrette over the asparagus. Sprinkle with the Parmesan cheese.

Let stand for 10 minutes or longer. Serve warm or at room temperature.

Serves 6   *Rie and Eddie Godsey, Meriwether's Market Restaurant*

Tomato Vinaigrette

1	tablespoon balsamic vinegar	1/2	cup olive oil
1 1/2	tablespoons fresh lemon juice	4	ounces fresh Italian plum tomatoes, finely chopped
1	teaspoon Dijon mustard	1/2	teaspoon salt
1/2	teaspoon minced garlic	1/4	teaspoon pepper

Combine the vinegar, lemon juice and Dijon mustard in a bowl and whisk until well blended. Stir in the garlic.

Add the olive oil gradually, whisking constantly until well blended. Stir in the tomato, salt and pepper.

Let stand at room temperature for 30 minutes or longer.

Makes 1 to 1 1/4 cups

Maple Hazelnut Bread

1 1/2 cups (about) hazelnuts
1 1/2 envelopes dry yeast
2   cups warm water
1/2   cup maple syrup

2 1/2 to 3 cups whole wheat flour
2 1/2 teaspoons salt
     Grated zest of 1 orange
1 1/2 to 2 cups all-purpose flour

Process the hazelnuts in a food processor until of the consistency of flour. Measure 1 cup of the hazelnut flour and set aside.

Combine the yeast, warm water and maple syrup in a large bowl and mix well. Let stand for 15 minutes.

Add the whole wheat flour, 1 cup hazelnut flour, salt and orange zest and mix well. Stir in the all-purpose flour 1/2 cup at a time until a stiff dough forms.

Turn the dough onto a lightly floured surface and knead until smooth and elastic. Place in a greased bowl, turning to coat the surface.

Let the dough rise, loosely covered, in a warm place until doubled in bulk.

Punch the dough down. Divide into 2 portions and shape into loaves. Place in 2 greased 5x9-inch loaf pans. Let rise, loosely covered, until doubled in bulk.

Bake at 375 degrees for 45 to 50 minutes or until golden brown and the loaves test done. Invert onto wire racks to cool.

Makes 2 loaves   *Lucia and Steve Coates, Montana Plains Bread Company*

Oak Ridge Estate, located in Nelson County, was built in 1802 by Robert Rives. The 23,000-square-foot mansion is part of a nearly 5,000-acre estate, which at one time also housed a blacksmith and carpentry shop, post office, power plant, ice plant, telephone company, telegraph station, school, and even its own train station. A previous owner, Thomas Fortune Ryan, was once listed as one of the ten wealthiest men in the United States. Born in nearby Lovingston, Ryan was a friend of Thomas Jefferson and hosted his contemporary on at least one overnight visit. Oak Ridge is privately owned but available by appointment for tours, festivals, and events.

Fried Banana Peppers with Jalapeño Cream Cheese

10	fresh banana peppers	1	(12-ounce) can beer
1⅓	cups flour	1	teaspoon hot sauce
2	tablespoons baking powder		Vegetable oil for deep-frying
1	teaspoon salt		Jalapeño Cream Cheese
½	teaspoon finely ground pepper		

Cut the banana peppers into halves and discard the seeds. Set the peppers aside.

Sift the flour, baking powder, salt and pepper into a bowl. Add the beer and hot sauce and mix well to make a batter. Add a small amount of water if necessary to make the batter of the desired consistency.

Dip the banana peppers into the batter. Cook in the oil in a deep fryer for 3 to 5 minutes or until golden brown, turning once. Drain on paper towels. If the batter does not stick to the peppers, rub the peppers lightly with olive oil and dust with flour before dipping into the batter.

Serve the banana peppers with the Jalapeño Cream Cheese. Garnish with black olives and whole grain mustard.

Serves 4 to 6   *France Burger, Café France*

Jalapeño Cream Cheese

24	ounces cream cheese, softened	½	cup minced green olives
½	cup minced pimentos or red bell pepper	1	to 3 jalapeños, minced
		2	teaspoons chopped fresh chives

Beat the cream cheese in a mixer bowl until smooth and creamy. Add the pimentos, olives, jalapeños and chives and mix well. Chill until serving time.

Cavalier Quiche

6	to 8 fresh mushrooms, sliced	2	deep-dish pie shells
1	tablespoon (about) butter	12	eggs
1	cup chopped fresh broccoli	4	cups whipping cream
1	cup shredded Cheddar cheese	3	tablespoons flour
1	cup shredded Swiss cheese	1	tablespoon salt

Sauté the mushrooms in the butter in a skillet until tender.

Place equal portions of the sautéed mushrooms, broccoli, Cheddar cheese and Swiss cheese in each pie shell.

Beat the eggs in a large bowl. Add the whipping cream, flour and salt and beat until smooth and well blended.

Pour about $1/4$ of the egg mixture over the ingredients in each pie shell, mixing gently; do not damage the pie pastry. Pour equal portions of the remaining egg mixture into each pie shell.

Bake at 300 degrees for 1 hour. Turn off the oven. Let the quiches stand in the closed oven for 30 minutes to set.

Remove the quiches. Let stand at room temperature to cool slightly. Cut into slices to serve.

Serves 12 to 16

Wells Duffy, The Cavalier

*Five-time Virginia governor Patrick Henry called **Red Hill**, his 2,920-acre plantation, "one of the garden spots of the world." Two of Henry's 17 children were born on the property and two were married there. Located near Brookneal, the plantation serves as a public memorial to Virginia's former statesman. The famous orator, well known for his "Give me liberty or give me death" decree, is buried on the property. Visitors to Red Hill can view the world's most extensive collection of Patrick Henry memorabilia.*

Corn Soufflé

4	eggs	1	cup frozen corn, thawed
1/4	cup flour	2	tablespoons melted butter
3/4	teaspoon salt	1 3/4	cups heavy cream
1/3	teaspoon white pepper		Grated Parmesan cheese

Beat the eggs in a medium bowl. Add the flour, salt and white pepper and beat until smooth and well blended. Stir in the corn, butter and cream.

Butter the bottom and side of a soufflé dish and dust lightly with Parmesan cheese. Pour the corn mixture into the prepared dish.

Bake at 350 degrees for 35 to 45 minutes or until the center is set.

Sprinkle with additional Parmesan cheese before serving.

Serves 10   *Molly and Ross Lynde, Hill City Grill*

Sweet Potato Soufflé

1	(16-ounce) can sweet potatoes	1/2	cup (1 stick) butter, softened
2	eggs, beaten	1	teaspoon nutmeg
2	cups sugar	1	teaspoon cinnamon
2	cups milk	1	teaspoon vanilla extract
			Chopped pecans

Drain the sweet potatoes and place in a large bowl. Mash the sweet potatoes well.

Add the eggs, sugar, milk and butter and mix until smooth and creamy. Mix in the nutmeg, cinnamon and vanilla. Pour into a greased baking dish.

Bake at 300 degrees for 45 minutes or until set.

Sprinkle chopped pecans over the top.

Serves 6 to 8   *Virginia Peaks of Otter Company, Peaks of Otter Lodge*

Potatoes au Gratin

2	pounds potatoes	1½	cups heavy cream
3	tablespoons unsalted butter		Salt and freshly ground
3	garlic cloves, chopped		pepper to taste

Peel and slice the potatoes thinly. Grease a 2-quart au gratin dish with the butter.

Sprinkle a small amount of garlic over the butter. Add a thin layer of the cream and a thin layer of the sliced potatoes.

Alternate layers of the cream and potatoes until all of the ingredients are used, sprinkling each layer of potatoes with salt and pepper and ending with a layer of cream.

Place the au gratin dish in a large shallow baking pan. Add a small amount of water to the large pan.

Bake at 350 degrees for 45 to 60 minutes or until the potatoes are tender and the top is well browned.

Serves 4 to 6　　　　　　　　　*Urs and Michelle Gabathuler, Main Street Eatery and Catering Company*

*The nineteenth-century rural community of Appomattox relied on the railroad for exchange of goods and services as well as information. The station house was vital to Appomattox residents' connection to other parts of the state and the world. The **Appomattox Train Station** marked the site of one of the Civil War's culminating battles. Brigadier General George Armstrong Custer intercepted three Confederate trains loaded with food and supplies intended to revitalize General Robert E. Lee's army. The ensuing battle resulted in Lee's surrender to General Ulysses S. Grant at Appomattox Court House and the end of the Civil War. No longer a functioning train station, the site houses the Appomattox Visitor Information Center and the Chamber of Commerce.*

Grilled Flank Steak with Chipotle-Honey Sauce

1	chipotle chile in adobo sauce, seeded, minced	1	tablespoon minced fresh cilantro
2	medium garlic cloves, minced	1	(2½-pound) flank steak
⅔	cup Key lime juice	1	teaspoon salt
		½	teaspoon pepper

Combine the chipotle chile, garlic, Key lime juice and cilantro in a large sealable plastic bag. Add the steak, close the bag and turn the bag to coat the steak with marinade. Refrigerate overnight, turning occasionally.

Preheat the grill. Drain the steak and discard the marinade. Sprinkle the steak with salt and pepper.

Place the steak on the grill. Grill for about 4 minutes on each side for medium rare, turning once. Remove the steak from the heat. Let stand for 5 minutes before slicing.

Slice the steak thinly across the grain diagonally. Serve as for fajitas with flour tortillas, red onion slices, avocado slices or guacamole and Chipotle-Honey Sauce with your favorite black bean dish on the side.

Serves 6   *Lucy Cook, Magnolia Foods*

Chipotle-Honey Sauce

4	chipotle chiles in adobo sauce, seeded	2	tablespoons balsamic vinegar
2	medium garlic cloves	2	tablespoons Dijon mustard
2	tablespoons chopped fresh cilantro leaves	½	cup Key lime juice
¼	cup honey	1	teaspoon ground cumin
2	tablespoons vegetable or canola oil		

Combine the chipotle chiles, garlic and cilantro in a food processor container and process until minced.

Add the honey, oil, vinegar, Dijon mustard, Key lime juice and cumin and pulse until well mixed.

May prepare the sauce a day ahead and refrigerate, covered, until serving time.

Almond and Coconut Lamb Curry

8	lamb rib chops	3	dried curry leaves
2	tablespoons olive oil	1/2	teaspoon ground cumin
1	medium onion, sliced	1/2	teaspoon turmeric
2	tablespoons olive oil	1	(5-ounce) can coconut milk
1	medium cooking apple, peeled, chopped	1	tablespoon ground almonds
2	medium carrots, chopped	1 1/4	cups slivered almonds, toasted
1	tablespoon chopped fresh cilantro leaves		

Trim the lamb chops, discarding the fat and bone. Cut the lamb into cubes.

Heat 2 tablespoons olive oil in a large heavy skillet over high heat. Add the lamb. Cook until brown, stirring frequently. Drain on paper towels.

Sauté the onion in 2 tablespoons olive oil in the skillet over medium heat until tender. Add the lamb, apple, carrots, cilantro, curry, cumin, turmeric and coconut milk. Bring to a boil, stirring frequently.

Simmer over low heat for 35 minutes or until the lamb is tender, stirring occasionally.

Stir in the ground almonds. Sprinkle the slivered almonds and additional curry over the top.

Serves 4 to 6

John Barthelmess, Oakwood Country Club

The **South River Meeting House**, commonly known as the Quaker Meeting House, served the area's Quaker population from its organization in 1757 until the late 1840s. The first log structure burned in 1768 and was replaced by a frame building, which soon became too small for the growing congregation. The existing stone structure was completed in 1798. The Presbyterians purchased the deteriorating building and ten acres of land from the Society of Friends in 1899. Following restoration in 1904, it was named the Quaker Memorial Presbyterian Church. Today, the Meeting House still stands on the church's property, but because of its status on both the Virginia and National historic registers, it is not used for church programs. City founder, John Lynch, is buried within the stonewalled cemetery.

Chicken Tostada Pizza

1/2	cup drained black beans	Chopped red onion
1/3	cup salsa	Shredded lettuce
1	(10-inch) pizza crust	Chopped tomatoes
1	(5-ounce) boneless skinless chicken breast, baked	Crushed tortilla chips
1/2	cup shredded Cheddar cheese	Ranch salad dressing
1/2	cup shredded Monterey Jack cheese	Additional salsa

Mix the black beans and 1/3 cup salsa in a bowl. Spread the mixture evenly over the pizza crust.

Chop the chicken breast. Sprinkle layers of the chicken, Cheddar cheese and Monterey Jack cheese over the black bean mixture. Place the crust on a baking sheet.

Bake at 350 degrees for 10 minutes or until the cheeses melt.

Place the pizza on a serving platter. Top with the desired amounts of red onion, lettuce, tomatoes and tortilla chips.

Cut the pizza into wedges. Serve with ranch salad dressing and additional salsa.

Serves 2

Eric Spain, Percival's Isle Java Tavern

Garlic Chicken

¹/₂	cup half-and-half	3	cups Alfredo sauce
¹/₂	cup vegetable oil	4	generous servings hot cooked
35	to 40 garlic cloves, chopped		linguini
3	cups julienned cooked		Grated Romano or Parmesan
	chicken		cheese
1	cup (heaping) broccoli		
	florets		

Combine the half-and-half, oil and garlic in a large saucepan. Cook over medium heat for several minutes. Add the chicken and broccoli. Sauté until heated through.

Add the Alfredo sauce. Cook until heated through, stirring constantly.

Add the linguini. Toss until the linguini is coated with the sauce and heated through.

Mound the pasta on plates or in pasta bowls. Sprinkle generously with Romano or Parmesan cheese.

Garnish with a sprinkle of freshly chopped parsley.

May substitute one 4-ounce jar chopped garlic for the 35 to 40 garlic cloves.

Serves 4

Abe McWane and Steve Hooten, Boodles

*A rare example of Greek Revival architecture, **Rivermont House** offers views of the James River and downtown Lynchburg. Located on Daniel's Hill, the mansion was built in 1857 during the decade in which the U.S. Census Bureau noted Lynchburg as the second wealthiest city per capita in the country. Judge William Daniel, Jr. built the home for Elizabeth Cabell, his second wife. Her name for the mansion, Rivermont, became the name of a real-estate company formed, in part, by a later owner of the home, Edward Sixtus Hutter. As a result of the Rivermont Company's development, the residential area several miles beyond the edge of downtown is now known as Rivermont, as is the bridge linking this early suburban area to the city center.*

Sesame Chicken

1	pound boneless skinless chicken breasts		1	cup diagonally sliced broccoli
1	egg			Teriyaki Sauce
1	cup cornstarch		1	(1-ounce) package sesame seeds
1/4	cup vegetable oil			
	Vegetable oil for deep-frying			

Cut the chicken into 1-inch cubes.

Beat the egg in a medium bowl. Add the cornstarch and 1/4 cup oil and beat until smooth. Add the chicken pieces and stir until coated. Let stand for several minutes.

Deep-fry the coated chicken pieces in 300-degree oil until golden brown. Drain on paper towels.

Blanch the broccoli for 2 to 3 minutes or just until tender-crisp.

Add the chicken and broccoli to the hot Teriyaki Sauce and stir gently until coated. Spoon the mixture onto a serving platter. Sprinkle with the sesame seeds.

Serves 2

Roger Tsuei, China Royal

Teriyaki Sauce

1/2	teaspoon chopped gingerroot		1/2	cup sugar
1/2	teaspoon minced garlic		1/4	cup cooking wine
1/4	cup soy sauce		1	teaspoon (about) cornstarch
1/4	cup vinegar		6	tablespoons chicken broth

Combine the gingerroot, garlic, soy sauce, vinegar, sugar and wine in a large saucepan over medium heat.

Dissolve enough cornstarch to thicken the sauce to the desired consistency in about half the chicken broth. Stir the remaining broth into the saucepan.

Bring the soy sauce mixture to a boil, stirring until the sugar dissolves completely.

Stir the cornstarch mixture into the saucepan. Cook until the sauce is clear and thickened, stirring constantly.

Kang Pao Chicken

10 to 12 ounces boneless skinless chicken legs	1 green onion
1 1/2 teaspoons cooking wine or sherry	1 1/2 teaspoons cooking wine or sherry
1 tablespoon soy sauce	2 tablespoons soy sauce
1 tablespoon cornstarch	2 tablespoons water
2 tablespoons vegetable oil	2 tablespoons sugar
1/2 cup vegetable oil for frying	1 1/2 tablespoons white vinegar
3 dried hot red peppers	1 1/2 tablespoons cornstarch
	Peanuts

Cut the chicken into 1-inch cubes. Combine 1 1/2 tablespoons wine, 1 tablespoon soy sauce and 1 tablespoon cornstarch in a medium bowl and mix well. Add the chicken pieces and stir until coated.

Mix in 1 tablespoon of the 2 tablespoons oil to help the chicken pieces separate easily during frying.

Preheat a wok or large heavy skillet. Add 1/2 cup oil and heat to frying temperature. Add the chicken. Stir-fry until cooked through. Remove the chicken to a plate and pour the oil from the wok.

Reheat the wok. Add remaining 1 tablespoon oil. Stir-fry the peppers in the hot oil over low heat until fragrant. Return the chicken to the wok. Slice the green onion into 10 pieces and add to the wok.

Blend 1 1/2 teaspoons wine, 2 tablespoons soy sauce, water, sugar, vinegar and cornstarch in a small bowl. Stir the mixture into the wok.

Cook over high heat until the chicken is glazed and heated to serving temperature, stirring constantly.

Add the desired amount of peanuts and toss lightly. Serve immediately.

Serves 4

Jean Hwang, King's Island

The **Booker T. Washington National Monument** commemorates the life and accomplishments of Booker Taliaferro Washington. Born a slave in 1856 on the Burroughs' tobacco farm in Franklin County, Washington attended college at the Hampton Institute. His 1901 autobiography, "Up from Slavery," distinguished him as a spokesman for his race. In addition to his accomplishments as an author, Dr. Booker T. Washington was an internationally recognized educator and orator.

Crook's Corner Shrimp

2 pounds peeled shrimp
10½ ounces bacon
1 tablespoon (about) peanut oil
4 cups sliced fresh mushrooms
3 cups sliced scallions
2 garlic cloves, pressed

2 tablespoons fresh lemon juice
Tabasco sauce to taste
Salt and pepper to taste
Chopped fresh parsley to taste

Rinse the shrimp and pat dry.

Chop the bacon. Cook in a large heavy skillet just until crisp, stirring frequently. Remove the bacon to paper towels to drain. Reserve the drippings in the skillet.

Add enough of the peanut oil to the drippings in the skillet to make a thin layer. Heat the drippings.

Add the shrimp to the skillet. Sauté the shrimp just until the color starts to change to pink. Add the mushrooms, scallions and garlic.

Sauté until the shrimp is cooked through and the mushrooms are tender. Stir in the lemon juice. Season with Tabasco sauce, salt, pepper and parsley.

Serve over Crook's Corner Creamy Grits (page 189).

Serves 8   *Rie and Eddie Godsey, Meriwether's Market Restaurnat*

Crook's Corner Creamy Grits

2 1/2 cups 2% milk
2 1/2 cups water
1   cup uncooked grits
1/2 teaspoon salt
1/4 cup margarine
1   cup shredded sharp Cheddar
     cheese

1/2 cup grated Parmesan cheese
1/8 teaspoon white pepper
1/8 teaspoon cayenne
1/8 teaspoon nutmeg

Combine the milk and water in a large saucepan. Bring the mixture to a boil.

Stir in the grits gradually. Reduce the heat.

Cook the grits for 20 minutes or until thick and creamy, stirring frequently and adding small amounts of additional water or milk as necessary to maintain the creamy consistency.

Add the salt, margarine, Cheddar cheese and Parmesan cheese and stir until the margarine and cheeses are melted and well blended with the grits.

Add the white pepper, cayenne and nutmeg and mix well.

Serves 6 to 7   *Rie and Eddie Godsey, Meriwether's Market Restaurnat*

One of Lynchburg's first houses, the **Miller-Claytor House**, sparked the creation of the Lynchburg Historical Society when the building's deterioration generated local preservation interest. In April of 1934, the Lynchburg Historical Society's first board, which consisted of representatives from the Junior League, the Lynchburg Garden Club, the Architects Club and the Art Club, convened to discuss the preservation of the eighteenth-century townhouse. The house was originally located on the corner of Eighth and Church Streets. It was purchased by the Historical Society in 1936, during Lynchburg's sesqui-centennial year, and moved to its present location near the entrance of Riverside Park. It operated as the Junior League headquarters from 1967 until 1985 when the League purchased its current headquarters on Rivermont Avenue.

Crab Cakes Welden

1/4	cup butter	1	egg, beaten
3	tablespoons flour	1	pound crab meat
1/8	teaspoon salt	1/3	cup chopped fresh parsley
2	tablespoons prepared mustard		Butter for frying
1/2	cup milk		Flour for dusting crab cakes

Melt the butter in a small saucepan. Add the flour and salt and blend well. Add the mustard and whisk until blended.

Whisk in the milk gradually. Cook for about 10 minutes or until the sauce thickens, whisking constantly.

Remove the sauce from the heat. Whisk a small amount of the hot sauce into the beaten egg; whisk the egg into the hot mixture. Whisk until smooth and well blended. Refrigerate the sauce.

Remove the sauce from the refrigerator about 30 minutes before making crab cakes.

Flake the crab meat in a bowl. Add the parsley and toss until well mixed. Add the sauce and mix lightly.

Shape the mixture by patting lightly into 2 1/2-inch cakes about 1/2 inch thick and place on waxed paper.

Melt about 2 tablespoons butter at a time in a large cast-iron skillet over medium heat. Dust the crab cakes lightly with flour and arrange the cakes around the side of the skillet and one in the center if space permits; do not crowd.

Cook until lightly browned on both sides, turning once. Remove to paper towels to drain. Repeat with remaining crab cakes.

The crab cakes are best served immediately but may be kept warm for 15 to 20 minutes if placed on a platter in a 100- to 125-degree oven. The cakes are also very good cold in sandwiches made with fresh white bread.

Serves 6 to 8   *Pepe Hughes, T.C. Trotters*

Crawfish Etouffé

1 tablespoon salt	³/₄ cup chopped yellow onion
1 tablespoon cayenne	³/₄ cup chopped celery
1 tablespoon white pepper	³/₄ cup chopped green bell
1 tablespoon black pepper	pepper
1 tablespoon basil leaves	8 cups shrimp stock
1¹/₂ teaspoons thyme leaves	3 cups chopped green onions
1¹/₂ cups vegetable oil	1¹/₂ cups unsalted butter
2 cups flour	2¹/₂ pounds crawfish tail meat

Combine the salt, cayenne, white pepper, black pepper, basil and thyme in a small bowl; mix well.

Heat the oil in a large saucepan over medium heat. Whisk the flour into the hot oil gradually, blending well. This mixture is the roux.

Cook the roux until the mixture turns the desired color ranging from tan to brown, stirring constantly. Be very careful as the mixture is extremely hot. Remove the roux from the heat when the desired color has been achieved.

Add the onion, celery, green pepper and seasoning mixture to the saucepan and mix well. Return to the heat and stir in the shrimp stock gradually. Cook over medium heat until the mixture thickens, stirring constantly.

Sauté the green onions in the butter in a skillet for about 1 minute. Stir the green onions and butter into the sauce and mix well. Bring the sauce to a boil, stirring occasionally. Reduce the heat. Simmer for 5 minutes, stirring occasionally.

Add the crawfish. Heat to serving temperature. Serve with hot cooked rice.

Serves 8   *Walter Hawkins, Jazz Street Grill*

Grilled Salmon on White Bean and Mushroom Ragout

1½	tablespoons fresh lemon juice	3	or 4 dashes of Tabasco sauce
2	tablespoons olive oil	10	(4-ounce) salmon fillets
⅛	teaspoon salt		White Bean and Mushroom
¼	teaspoon pepper		Ragout
⅔	teaspoon dried dillweed	¼	cup chopped fresh parsley

Combine the lemon juice, olive oil, salt, pepper, dillweed and Tabasco sauce in a small bowl and mix well. Pour a thin layer of the marinade into a shallow dish. Dip the salmon fillets into the marinade to coat on both sides. Arrange the fillets on a preheated oiled griddle or barbecue grill. Cook for 3 to 5 minutes.

Brush the fillets with the remaining marinade; turn the fillets over. Cook for about 3 minutes longer or until the salmon flakes easily.

Ladle the White Bean and Mushroom Ragout into soup plates. Sprinkle with the parsley and place a salmon fillet on top.

Serves 10   *Rie and Eddie Godsey, Meriwether's Market Restaurant*

White Bean and Mushroom Ragout

1	pound fresh mushrooms	2	tablespoons olive oil
2	teaspoons minced garlic	2	pounds dried cannellini
½	cup chopped red onion		(white kidney) beans, cooked
1	pound red or yellow bell peppers, chopped	1	cup white wine
2	teaspoons salt	½	cup water
½	teaspoon pepper	8	ounces fresh tomatoes, chopped

Brush the mushrooms carefully with a mushroom brush or towel to clean. Cut the larger mushrooms into halves or ½-inch slices and leave the smaller mushrooms whole. Regular mushrooms, shiitake, cremini or other assorted wild mushrooms are suitable for this recipe.

Sauté the mushrooms, garlic, onion, bell peppers, salt and pepper in the olive oil in a large skillet for 3 minutes or until the mushrooms are lightly browned.

Drain and rinse the beans. Add to the mushroom mixture. Stir in the wine, tomatoes and water. Cook for 3 minutes or until the mushrooms are tender and the beans are heated through.

Adjust the seasonings and keep warm until serving time.

Apple Dapple Cake

2 cups sugar
1 1/2 cups vegetable oil
3 eggs
3 cups flour
1 teaspoon salt
1 teaspoon baking soda
2 teaspoons cinnamon

3 cups chopped apples
1 cup chopped nuts
2 cups coconut
1/2 cup margarine
1 cup packed brown sugar
1/4 cup milk

Combine the sugar, oil and eggs in a large bowl and beat until the mixture is light and fluffy.

Sift the flour, salt, baking soda and cinnamon together. Add to the sugar mixture and beat until well blended.

Fold in the apples, nuts and coconut. Pour into a greased and floured 9x13-inch cake pan.

Bake at 350 degrees for 45 minutes or until the cake tests done.

Combine the margarine, brown sugar and milk in a saucepan. Heat until the mixture is smooth and well blended, stirring constantly. Bring to a boil and boil for 2 minutes.

Pour the hot mixture over the hot cake. Cool in the pan on a wire rack.

Serves 12 to 15

Perkins Flippin, The Farm Basket

Built in 1871, **Bragassa's Store** was the first building in Lynchburg to feature plate-glass windows. Francisco Bragassa undertook the building and creation of Bragassa's Store, a toy store and bakery shop, with money he had made in the California Gold Rush. The bakery was eventually discontinued, but three generations of Bragassas owned and operated the toy store. The Lynchburg Historical Foundation purchased the former toy store in 1988, and its offices are on the second floor of the completely restored building.

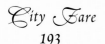

White Fruitcake

8	ounces figs		Flour to coat fruits and nuts
8	ounces citron	2	cups butter, softened
2	pounds candied pineapple	1	pound sugar
1	pound candied cherries	12	egg yolks, beaten
2	pounds white raisins	3½	cups flour
2	pounds pecan halves	1	large glass whiskey
1	pound whole almonds	12	egg whites, stiffly beaten

Line a 10-inch tube pan with heavily greased white paper.

Cut the figs, citron, candied pineapple and candied cherries into desired size pieces. Combine all the fruits and nuts in a large bowl. Add enough flour to coat, tossing to coat.

Cream the butter and sugar in a very large bowl until light and fluffy. Add the egg yolks and beat until well blended. Add the flour and whiskey alternately, mixing well after each addition.

Fold in the stiffly beaten egg whites. Stir in the fruit and nut mixture.

Pack the mixture firmly into the prepared tube pan.

Bake at 300 degrees for 2 hours or until the cake tests done. Cool in the pan on a wire rack for several minutes.

Invert onto a wire rack to cool completely.

Serves 16 to 20   *Perkins Flippin, The Farm Basket*

Crème Brûlée

4	cups whipping cream	1/8	teaspoon salt
1/4	cup sugar	8	egg yolks
1	tablespoon vanilla extract		Brown sugar

Combine the whipping cream, sugar, vanilla and salt in a large heavy saucepan over low heat.

Bring the mixture to 180 to 185 degrees to scald the cream, stirring occasionally.

Beat the egg yolks in a stainless steel bowl until thick and lemon colored. Stir a small amount of the scalded cream mixture into the egg yolks to temper. Stir the remaining hot cream mixture into the egg yolks gradually; do not beat. The mixture should not foam.

Pour the egg mixture into ten 6-ounce ramekins. Arrange the ramekins in a large baking pan. Add enough water to the pan to come halfway up the ramekins.

Bake in a preheated 350-degree oven for 25 to 30 minutes or until a knife inserted 1 inch from the edge of the custard comes out clean; the centers will be soft.

Remove the ramekins from the baking pan and place on a wire rack to cool completely. Cover the ramekins and refrigerate overnight.

Preheat the broiler. Sift 1/4 inch of brown sugar evenly over the top of each custard.

Place the ramekins 6 to 8 inches from the heat source. Broil for 1 to 2 minutes or until the brown sugar melts, turning if necessary for even melting. Return the ramekins to the refrigerator immediately.

Serve very cold. The crust will hold for up to 6 hours.

Serves 10   *Rie and Eddie Godsey, Meriwether's Market Restaurant*

Pumpkin Cheesecake

32   ounces cream cheese, softened
1½   cups sugar
½   teaspoon cinnamon
¼   teaspoon ginger
⅛   teaspoon ground cloves

1   (15-ounce) can pumpkin
4   eggs
2   teaspoons vanilla extract
    Pecan Graham Cracker Crust
    Cinnamon Whipped Cream

Combine the cream cheese, sugar, cinnamon, ginger and cloves in a large bowl and beat until smooth and creamy. Add the pumpkin and beat until smooth. Add the eggs 1 at a time, beating until smooth after each addition. Beat in the vanilla. Pour the cream cheese mixture into the Pecan Graham Cracker Crust. Place the springform pan in a larger baking pan. Add water to the pan to a depth of 1 inch.

Bake in a preheated 350-degree oven for 1 hour and 45 minutes or until the top is golden brown and a knife inserted in the center comes out clean.

Remove the springform pan to a wire rack to cool. Cover the springform pan and refrigerate overnight. Loosen the cheesecake from the side of the pan and remove the side of the pan. Place the cheesecake on a serving plate. Top with the Cinnamon Whipped Cream.

Serves 10 to 12   *Brad Barden, Boonsboro Country Club*

Pecan Graham Cracker Crust

½   cup pecans, finely chopped
1   cup graham cracker crumbs

¼   cup sugar
5   tablespoons melted butter

Combine the pecans, graham cracker crumbs and sugar in a bowl and toss to mix well. Add the butter and mix well. The mixture should have the consistency of wet sand. Press the mixture evenly over the bottom of a 9-inch springform pan.

Bake at 350 degrees for 10 minutes. Wrap the bottom and side of the pan with foil to make it watertight.

Cinnamon Whipped Cream

1   cup heavy whipping cream
¼   cup confectioners' sugar

1   teaspoon vanilla extract
1   teaspoon cinnamon

Combine the whipping cream, confectioners' sugar, vanilla and cinnamon in a small bowl. Beat at low speed until well blended. Beat at high speed until stiff peaks form.

Raspberry Orange Pie

1/4	cup butter, softened	1	teaspoon grated orange zest
1	cup sugar	2	cups fresh or frozen
2	tablespoons flour		raspberries
3	eggs	1	unbaked (9-inch) pie shell
1	cup freshly squeezed orange juice		

Combine the butter and sugar in a large bowl and whisk until well blended. Add the flour and whisk until smooth.

Add the eggs 1 at a time, whisking until smooth and well blended after each addition. Whisk in the orange juice and zest gradually.

Fold in the raspberries gently.

Pour the raspberry mixture into the pie shell.

Bake in a preheated 425-degree oven for 15 minutes.

Reduce the oven temperature to 375 degrees. Bake for 35 to 45 minutes longer or until the crust is golden brown and the filling shakes like gelatin.

Place the pie on a wire rack to cool.

Serves 6 to 8　　　　　*Lucia and Steve Coates, Montana Plains Bread Company*

*Martin Luther King, Jr., Booker T. Washington, George Washington Carver, and Thurgood Marshall are among those who visited Lynchburg poet and co-founder of the local NAACP chapter, **Anne Bethel Spencer**, at her 1313 Pierce Street residence. This Queen Anne-style home, built in 1903, was the poet's residence for most of her adult life. Her husband, Edward, built the backyard detached study for Anne, calling it Edankraal: Edan, a combination of the couple's first names and kraal, the African word for dwelling. The property is maintained, and opened by appointment to the public, as a memorial to the Dunbar High School librarian who was Virginia's first African-American woman to be published in the first edition of the Norton Anthology of Modern Poetry.*

Crème Fraîche

1 cup heavy cream
1 teaspoon buttermilk

Pour the cream into a small saucepan. Blend in the buttermilk. Heat the mixture to lukewarm, not over 85 degrees. Pour the warm mixture into a loosely covered jar. Let stand at room temperature (between 60 and 85 degrees) until the mixture is thickened. Stir the mixture, cover and store in the refrigerator.

Tarte Tatin (Apple Tart)

4 *pounds (about 9) firm cooking apples*	1/2 *cup sugar*
1/3 *cup sugar*	6 *tablespoons melted butter*
1 *teaspoon cinnamon*	*Pâte Brisée Sucrée*
2 *tablespoons butter, softened*	*Crème Fraîche*

Peel and core the apples and cut into 1/8-inch slices. Place the apples in a large bowl. Add 1/3 cup sugar and cinnamon and toss until the slices are coated.

Butter a 2-quart glass baking dish generously with the softened butter. Sprinkle half the 1/2 cup sugar in the bottom of the buttered dish. Arrange 1/3 of the apples in the baking dish and drizzle with 1/3 of the melted butter. Repeat with 2 more layers of the remaining apples and butter. Sprinkle the remaining 1/4 cup sugar over the top.

Roll the pastry on a lightly floured surface into a circle the size of the top of the baking dish. Place the pastry over the apples and tuck the edge inside the rim of the baking dish. Cut four or five 1/8-inch vents in the pastry.

Place the baking dish in the lower third of a preheated 400-degree oven. Bake for 1 hour or until the juices have cooked into a thick brown syrup that is visible when the baking dish is tilted. Cover lightly with foil if the pastry begins to brown too quickly.

Invert the tart onto an ovenproof serving dish immediately.

If the apples have not turned a light caramel color, sprinkle the apples with a small amount of confectioners' sugar and broil for several minutes until the surface is caramelized. Serve the tart warm with Crème Fraîche.

Serves 8   *Lucy Cook, Magnolia Foods*

Pâte Brisée Sucrée (Pastry)

1 1/3 *cups flour*	3 *tablespoons Crisco shortening, chilled*
2 *tablespoons sugar*	5 *to 6 tablespoons cold water*
1/4 *teaspoon salt*	
1/2 *cup butter, chilled*	

Combine the flour, sugar and salt in a food processor container. Pulse several times to mix. Add the butter and shortening and pulse until the mixture is crumbly. Add 5 tablespoons water all at once and process until the mixture forms a ball, adding additional water several drops at a time if necessary.

Wrap the pastry in plastic wrap. Let stand for 3 hours.

Celebrations

Friday Cheers

A Cocktail Party for a Crowd

Is the day-in, day-out 9-to-5 grind starting to get to you? Looking for a way to build workplace camaraderie or reward employees for a job well done? Take advantage of our Friday Cheers menu, and create a quick and easy party for week's end.

Virtually all of this menu can be prepared a day or two ahead, making it ideal for a home where both adults work. On your way home, pick up your favorite chicken tenders or wings and fresh tortilla chips for the salsa. For a different twist, try serving a good bottled bleu cheese dressing as dip for the chicken tenders. Now's the time to make use of all the wacky serving dishes and margarita glasses you've been collecting. And pull out those funny cocktail napkins you've been keeping in the drawer!

Spread the word, mix the margaritas, and have the gang over for an hour or an evening—the weekend is here!

Great for a get-together while watching the ACC Tournament or as a pre-game party for your favorite teenagers. For the young crowd, just substitute sodas and juices, and invite them to stop by before they head to the kickoff.

Friday Cheers *is an annual, outside summer concert series presented by Lynch's Landing, Inc. Held every two weeks from May through August at the Lynchburg Community Market, the event provides an opportunity for socializing, dancing, and relaxing in Lynchburg's unique downtown atmosphere. A different regional band performs a wide variety of music for each Friday Cheers. As a nonprofit organization focused on promoting downtown revitalization, Lynch's Landing, Inc. shares Friday Cheers' profits with other similar organizations committed to improving downtown Lynchburg.*

Photograph on overleaf:
Thomas Jefferson's Poplar Forest
by Robert DeVaul

Red, White, and Hot!

A Fourth of July Picnic at Poplar Forest

What better place to spend a patriotic July 4th than Poplar Forest, Thomas Jefferson's retreat home! This child-friendly menu will ensure that both children and adults have a great time. The entire picnic can be made and/or purchased the day before and takes advantage of the abundance of fresh summer vegetables and fruits. Pack your picnic basket with a red checked cloth and red and blue paper plates. Don't forget plastic cups for the Gazpacho and tea!

While the children play games on the lawn, the adults can enjoy cold Gazpacho and sandwiches. When the children are worn out, Fruit Kabobs, sandwiches, and Peanut Butter Oatmeal Bars will be a hit.

As evening approaches, pack up and head off to your favorite fireworks watching spot for a dramatic ending to a fun-filled day.

*During the construction of **Poplar Forest**, Thomas Jefferson's personal retreat, Jefferson wrote, "When finished, it will be the best dwelling house in the state, except that of Monticello; perhaps preferable to that, as more proportioned to the faculties of a private citizen." In 1806, on land he had inherited from his father-in-law, John Wyles, Jefferson built his retreat in a unique octagonal design, complete with elaborate landscaping. The working plantation spread over 4,812 acres, with cash crops of tobacco, corn, and wheat. The former president journeyed to Poplar Forest several times each year. Today, in addition to viewing ongoing restoration, visitors can observe archaeological digs. The Corporation for Jefferson's Poplar Forest, a nonprofit organization, aims to preserve and restore the property for the cultural and educational benefit of the public.*

Mileposts

A Graduation Brunch for 10 to 12

Cream Cheese Bran Muffins	*page 48*
Tossed Fruit Salad	
Sausage and Wild Rice Casserole	*page 55*
Committee Coffee Cake	*page 41*
Chilled Orange and Grapefruit Juices	
Coffee and Tea	

Honor your graduate with a casual gathering during this very special time. With graduation parties, cookouts, and beach trips filling up busy schedules, a brunch gives you a fighting chance to share in their excitement and catch up on their plans for the future. Double the recipes as needed to accommodate the number of guests. Combine your favorite cut up fruits with torn Bibb lettuce and poppy seed dressing for a light and colorful addition to the meal.

Allow the graduates to serve themselves by placing a stack of plates (in school colors, of course!) at the start of the buffet line and cutlery and napkins at the end. Offer juices and coffee and tea in a different area to avoid congestion. Or, if weather permits, set up tables in your yard for the buffet and patio chairs for the graduates. Above all, take time to enjoy their company before the graduates move on to the next milepost!

Consider this menu for serving out-of-town relatives and friends the morning after a wedding. At this point, folks are more relaxed and will enjoy reflecting on the wedding. Send them home with good memories and a great meal!

The Lynchburg area is abundant with institutions of higher learning. Two women's colleges, Sweet Briar and Randolph-Macon Woman's College, and a third private institution, Lynchburg College, offer four-year degrees in the liberal arts. Two Christian colleges, Liberty University and The Virginia University of Lynchburg, offer degrees as well. Central Virginia Community College offers a two-year degree, and many CVCC students transfer their credits or participate in Old Dominion University's extended-degree program. Additionally, area students can obtain transferable credits from The University of Virginia's Extension program. Two business colleges, Miller-Motte and National Business College, offer two-year degrees in business-related disciplines. Graduate degrees are available to qualified participants through Lynchburg College and Liberty University. The colleges offer an enticing array of guest speakers, performances, sporting events, and community activities to the public.

Friends, Food, and Fun!

A Supper Club Buffet for 10

The next time it's your turn to host a supper club dinner, try this cocktail buffet instead of the traditional sit-down dinner. As they nibble, your guests will have more freedom to mingle. This might be a great time to invite some new folks to join your supper club.

Choose to make the entire menu yourself (much can be prepared ahead) or pass along individual recipes to supper club members for preparation. Serve the tenderloin with horseradish sauce, mustard, and crusty rolls.

As guests enjoy dessert and coffee, take a friendly vote on everyone's favorite dish and plan the next supper club date!

Supper Clubs *are a popular way to get together with friends while experimenting with new recipes or showcasing culinary skill. Many supper clubs have themes to pull the gathering together. Some are black-tie affairs, while others invite the more casual look. Members of a supper club typically share the responsibilities for the meal. Some have the host couple prepare the main course and assign other members specific dishes as accompaniments. Others make general suggestions but leave the choice of the recipe to the cook. Supper clubs whose focus is culinary distinction may cook some dishes ahead of time but prepare one dish together in the host's kitchen. The only essential ingredient is food; other requirements are at the whim of the participants!*

It's A Girl! (or Boy!)

A Christening Buffet for 10

Celebration Punch	page 36
Baked Ham	
Fiesta Cheese Grits	page 70
Broccoli Crunch Salad (double recipe)	page 24
Sweet Potato Smoothie	page 68
Bakery Dinner Rolls	
Heavenly Hummingbird Cake	page 128

A new baby is always a cause for celebration! Relatives and friends are in town for the occasion. This menu makes it easy for the new mother to entertain in style and still keep her sanity! Purchase your favorite ham and dinner rolls (buy an extra dozen to make ham rolls the next day) and prepare the grits, sweet potatoes, and cake the day before the big event.

Set up the buffet on your sideboard or kitchen counter, allowing guests to eat at your dining table. If you place flowers in the church in honor of the day, consider using them as your centerpiece. Serve the ham at room temperature, and while the grits and sweet potatoes are warming in the oven, share a toast to the new baby and godparents with Celebration Punch. Toss the dressing with the Broccoli Crunch Salad at the last minute. Heavenly Hummingbird Cake is an elegant and appropriate finish for welcoming the new arrival.

This menu would also make a special Christmas dinner.

It's Lobster Time!

A Lobster Party for 6

Boiled Lobster or	
Steamed Lobster	*page 115*
Drawn Butter	*page 115*
Marinated Coleslaw	*page 26*
Pumpkin Dump Cake	*page 152*

The Junior League's annual lobster sale presents a wonderful opportunity to throw a casual supper for close friends. Although appearing decadent, a lobster supper is actually a simple way to entertain, and our easy lobster preparations will make you feel you're at the seashore no matter what time of year it is! Drawn Butter is the traditional accompaniment; however, try just a squirt of fresh lemon for a lighter taste. Marinated Coleslaw adds texture and color and is easily made ahead.

A lobster supper calls for a casual atmosphere. Use brown paper or comics on your kitchen or picnic table and scatter the shells from your beach trip last summer across it. Give your guests plastic lobster bibs or brightly colored kitchen dishtowels to protect their clothes and dig in!

Eating lobster is a deliciously sensual experience. So order up plenty of lobster and call your best friends for a wonderfully simple feast!

*The Junior League of Lynchburg sponsors an annual **Lobster Sale** as one means of raising funds for its community projects. The Junior League addresses community needs by researching possible solutions and responding with projects. Past projects of the League include the establishment of the Adult Day Care Center; Amazement Square, a children's museum; and Kids' Haven, a center for grieving children. Other projects are ongoing, such as Day in the Park and Children's Theatre. More recently, the League has begun working in coalition with other non-profit organizations to combine efforts. A homeless shelter for teen mothers and a community health center are examples of these partnerships.*

Congratulations!

A Celebration Dinner for 8

Jim's Oysters (**use appetizer servings**)	page 116
Orange and Romaine Salad with Feisty Salad Dressing	page 31
Filets Mignons with Shiitake Madeira Sauce	page 78
James River Rice	page 70
Company Carrots	page 60
Vanilla Ice Cream with Crunchy Topping	page 149
Saint Hilaire Champagne	

Whether it's a promotion, a birthday, an engagement, or welcoming newcomers to town, you are ready to celebrate. This menu allows you to prepare a "meal to remember" while at the same time enjoying your guests. The salad dressing, rice, and ice cream topping can be prepared ahead, leaving only the oysters and filets for the last minute.

This is the time to make your dining room sparkle by pulling out the china and crystal. Use lots of candles and your best table linens, and scatter silver or gold confetti on the table.

Chill the Champagne and get ready to celebrate!

The Finish Line

An "After the Ten-Miler" Dinner for 8

Tequila Marinated Shrimp and	*page 9*
Herb Focaccia	*page 7*
Bloody Mary Chili *(double recipe)*	*page 18*
Tossed Green Salad with *Your Favorite Dressing*	
Corn Bread *("Jiffy" mixes can't be beat!)*	
Sinful Chocolate Chess Pie	*page 145*
Assorted Chilled Beers *and Waters*	

They've made it up "Farm Basket Hill" and had an afternoon rest—now it's time to get together and celebrate how much better they did than last year! While everyone is resting weary bones and discussing times, pass Tequila Marinated Shrimp and Herb Focaccia. Depending on the weather (sometimes it is still quite warm on Ten-Miler Day), serve dinner on your patio or deck. Use bandanas for napkins, and serve the soup in crocks with plenty of warm corn bread and softened butter. Sinful Chocolate Chess Pie is an indulgent end to a tiring but satisfying day!

This menu also works well for a Super Bowl Party. Simply set up TV trays or small tables for each person in your family room. Serve, and enjoy the cheers from your fans!

The **Virginia Ten-Miler** has been a Lynchburg tradition since 1974. The annual foot race attracts world-class runners and has included several Olympic medalists. The racecourse goes through business districts and residential sections as it winds from E.C. Glass High School to Rivermont Avenue, passing Randolph-Macon Woman's College and looping through Riverside Park. "Farm Basket Hill," the final stretch of the race, is a popular place to cheer on the road-weary. Runners report that the enthusiasm from the crowds has motivated them along the race's final leg from The Farm Basket to the finish line at E.C. Glass.

A Day at the Races

A Tailgate Picnic at Point-to-Point

Sustainer Cheese Straws	*page 6*
French Mushroom Soup or Chilled Cucumber Soup	*pages 169 and 21*
Pecan-Crusted Chicken with Mustard Sauce (make with chicken tender pieces for ease of serving)	*page 104*
Black Bean and Corn Salad	*page 25*
Crusty Baguettes	
Grandma's Molasses Cookies	*page 137*
Sliced Apples	
Apple Cider	

The Point-to-Point races are a wonderful way to spend an autumn afternoon. Whether the day is warm or cool, the menu above can be adapted for the occasion. If the day is crisp and cool, serve the French Mushroom Soup and heat the cider (these are easily transported in large thermoses). On a warm day, the Chilled Cucumber Soup and cold cider are refreshing.

Take along brightly colored pottery, a potted fall mum, and a colorful cloth or blanket to cover your tailgate. After your guests have enjoyed the meal, pass Grandma's Molasses Cookies with crisp fall apple slices from your favorite local orchard to top off the day.

Delicious for tailgating at your next college football game as well.

*Wolf Branch Farm, on the historic Radford Estate, is the site of the annual **Old-Fashioned Point-to-Point** horse races. The six races, held on the second Sunday of October, raise funds to benefit the Bedford Hunt Club. In addition to the races, contests include a hunter-pace event over fences, a stick pony race for children, terrier races, and tailgate competitions. Thousands of visitors gather to watch and participate in the races and enjoy what is noted as one of the area's favorite views of the Peaks of Otter and adjacent Blue Ridge Mountains. A large portion of the race site has recently been protected in a conservation easement, recorded with the Virginia Outdoors Foundation, which will ensure that generations of Central Virginians will continue to appreciate the expanse of rolling farmland and bordering mountain ridges.*

It's Springtime!

A Garden Day Luncheon for 6

Greek Chicken Breasts	*page 99*
Fiesta Fruit Salad	*page 23*
Steamed White Rice with Peas	
Coconut Pound Cake	*page 125*
Iced Tea and Coffee	

Take a break from touring the homes and gardens of Virginia with this make-ahead luncheon. The chicken breasts can bake while you tour one more home, and the rice can be prepared in 20 minutes while your guests enjoy iced tea and discuss the gardens they've seen. (Add a handful of frozen green peas to your rice midway through cooking for springtime color.)

If the weather cooperates (and doesn't it always on Garden Day!), have lunch outdoors on your patio or deck. Cover a round table with a to-the-floor flowered cloth and set it with pure white china or crockery. A casual arrangement of tulips and lilac from your garden makes a fragrant centerpiece. After cake and coffee, it's off to the next home on the tour!

Wonderful for a bridesmaid's luncheon or baby shower.

Lynchburg participates annually in the Garden Club of Virginia's **Historic Garden Week**. *Area garden clubs, led by the Hillside and Lynchburg Garden Clubs, host visitors at a variety of privately owned homes and gardens during Garden Day. Proceeds from the events support the Garden Club of Virginia's restoration of historic gardens. Among those restored are gardens at Point of Honor, the University of Virginia's Rotunda, and the forecourt in front of the Lee Chapel at Washington and Lee University.*

The **Lynchburg Symphony Orchestra** was incorporated in 1983 through the efforts of area musicians. The Symphony comprises both professional and local musicians who perform seven concerts each year, two of which are designated as youth concerts. Additionally, members of the music community, youth and adults alike, benefit from master classes with guest artists. A local foundation makes possible an annual free summer concert, offered outdoors and often accompanied by fireworks and other attractions.

Encore, Encore!

An After-the-Symphony Dessert Party

Five-Flavor Pound Cake	*page 126*
Raspberry Shortbread	*page 140*
Sallie's Chocolate Tarts	*page 141*
Caroline's Praline Bars	*page 135*
Cheese Pennies	*page 6*
Deep-Dish Buttermilk Cheesecake	*page 130*
Regular and Decaffeinated Coffee	
Assorted Liqueurs and Cordials	

A dessert party is an easy and elegant way to entertain a large group of people, and what better time than after the Symphony! Selections and quantities of these recipes can be altered to suit the size of your crowd. The Buttermilk Cheesecake is very rich, so remember to cut small wedges.

Place the Raspberry Shortbread and Praline Bars in your hallway or living room as pickup goodies as guests arrive (don't forget the napkins!). This will also encourage your guests to circulate. The Pound Cake, Tarts, and Cheesecake can be placed on your dining room table, along with a stack of pretty dessert plates (mix and match if you are a china collector) and dessert forks. Serve coffee and liqueurs from decorative trays on your sideboard or your kitchen table, along with cream, sugar cubes, and pretty cordial glasses. Frangelica, Raspberry Chambord, Amaretto, Cointreau, and Bailey's Irish Cream are just a few of the wonderful liqueurs available, all great on their own or in concert with coffee.

A dessert party is also a fun way to include husbands in a bridal or baby shower.

Time For Two

Picnic on the Parkway

Greek Pita Pockets	*page 28*
Sweet Red Pepper Soup	*page 171*
Artichoke and Rice Salad (half recipe)	*page 24*
Baguettes and Brie Cheese	
Brownies with Mint Frosting	*page 132*
Chilled Pinot Grigio or Gewürztraminer	

With busy lives and little ones in need of attention, sometimes we must actively plan to spend time with our spouses. Schedule a "date," pack a picnic, and head up to your favorite spot on the Blue Ridge Parkway, no matter what the season. If it's chilly, add a thermos of Sweet Red Pepper Soup and substitute hot chocolate or coffee for the Pinot Grigio.

Prepare the Greek veggies ahead and assemble the pita pockets at the picnic. Take along a thick blanket or throw for picnicking in a sunny spot. Allow the Brie to soften, uncork the wine, and enjoy each other's company!

Can't get away? Enjoy the picnic in front of your fireplace after the children are snug in their beds.

For a child-friendly picnic menu, see Red, White, and Hot! in this chapter.

Central Virginia's scenic mountains form part of the 470-mile **Blue Ridge Parkway**. Construction of the Parkway began in 1935 near the Virginia-North Carolina border and ended in 1987 with the completion of North Carolina's Grandfather Mountain segment. Its purpose was to link Virginia's Shenandoah National Park and the North Carolina Smoky Mountain National Park with a recreationally oriented motorway. The natural and cultural histories of the Appalachian Mountains are preserved and interpreted along the parkway with access to more than 250 overlook areas and information on nearly 100 bird species. Called the "backbone" of the mountain region, the Parkway covers an area of approximately 20,000 square miles, providing a home to a variety of wildlife, including bobcats, foxes, deer, and black bears. More than 100 million travelers visit the Blue Ridge Parkway each year.

Steering Committee

Chairman	*Historical Text Chairman*
Helen F. Wheelock	Nina Vest Salmon
Assistant Chairman	*Art and Design Chairman*
Courtney Banton Alford	Rebecca Gentry
Recipe Chairman	*Treasurer*
Ingrid J. McCrary	Pamela S. Bradford
Marketing Chairman	*Sustainer Advisor*
Natalie DuBose Langley	Jane Frost Bowden

Assistant Recipe Chairman	*Promotions Chairman*
Beverly Twitty	Katherine Brant Manning
Assistant Marketing Chairman and	*Special Events Chairmen*
Corporate Sales Chairman	Ashley Flynn Blanchard
Laura R. Casler	Caren Harvey
	Mary Beth Hunter
Retail Sales Co-Chairmen	Dayna Evans Taylor
Robin Naisawald Edson	
Esther S. McGuinn	

Contributors

Special Thanks

The efforts of the active and provisional members of the Junior League of Lynchburg made this cookbook a reality. Their dedication to contributing and testing recipes, researching and composing text, designing and coordinating artwork, and marketing the book is exhibited throughout.

Lisa K. Aft

Miranda Ison Alston

Jennifer Purdie Anderson

Beth Andrus

Pam Bailey

Sherry Cristina Baldwin

Deborah M. Baroch

Susan Page Bingham

Brenda L. Blanchette

Laura Maurer Blondino

Linda Via Boylan

Hollis Bradley

Julie Hatcher Brammer

Laura Gambacorta
    Brawley

Mary E. Burgess

Angie Campbell

Becky Campbell

Teresa F. Campbell

Ashley Hoskins
    Carrington

Laura Glass Coleman

Allison N. Cox

Nicolle R. Cundiff

Sandra Davidson

Katherine DeRosear

Pavlina Dirom

Mary Kett Driskill

Linda Gibson Duerson

Amanda Eberwine

Belle Evans

Shawne Murphy Farmer

Landon W. Fauber

Laura O. Frey

Ginny Frings

Patricia H. Garner

Anne Garrard

Kennon Giles

Elizabeth Bone Goolsby

Christine Gries

Judi Handel

M. Allegra Helms

Jane Marie Henderson

Caroline Howard Heppner

Ann DeVerter Holland

Jane L. Hope

Kimberly Hopkins

Susan Hudson

Claudia S. Hunt

Lane Jackson

Carter Fauber Jennings

Betsy Johnson

Elizabeth M. Walker
    Johnson

Laurie Joyner

Lee Pat Bowen Kelleher

Allison Kughn

Maren H. Leggett

Shawn C. Lipscomb

Kristine Lloyd

Elizabeth W. Lovern

Pattie Martin

Mary Matson

Dia Mays

Sheryl Kingery Mays

Anne Tyler B. McCabe

Jennifer Huntley McCarthy

Tina McLaughlin

Rebecca Michie McVeigh

Anna McWane

Colleen Miller

Angela Cline Morris

Carol A. Morris
Kelly Piggott
   Mortemousque
Beth Estill Mullen
Renee Nail
Kelli Sanford Pacheco
Brooke B. Pettyjohn
Claudia B. Pierpoint
Sharon Pinkston
Jennifer Price
Tammie A. Pyle

Pamela Wilson Reams
Kakie Saunders Richards
Susan Richards
Maria Roberts
Anne G. Royer
Blake T. Royer
Angela R. Russell
Nicole Barbour Sawyer
Debra Serio
Aimee Brantley Shenigo
Catherine K. Shircliff

Michelle M. Sisk
Jaleh K. Slominski
Jennifer Monroe Smith
Sarah Smith
Sarah C. Sorenson
Tina St. John
Mary Lou Stufano
Sonia Terrell
Teresa Turner-Hall
Mary Armbrister Tyrey
Lalla S. Wood

Also, many of our sustaining members contributed their favorite recipes and supported us with their wisdom, experience, and enthusiasm.

Susan G. Ackley
Eleanor Neas Atkins
Deidre Atwill
Betty S. Brown
Norvell N. Carrington
Rondys Trent Cook
Sarah Gurkin Craddock
Laura Bullock Crumbley
Catherine Dalton
Kandy Elliott
Marion Love Farmer
Dona P. Forehand
Linda Franke
Katherine M. Gray
Cornelia B. Harbison

Nancy Heilman-Davis
Ellie H. Hubbard
Karen L. Hyde
Mary Ellen Inman
Frances H. Jackson
Wendee Kramen
Kristine Kughn
Margie Lippard
Langhorne Lewis
   McCarthy
Catherine S. McGehee
Sarah Moore
Karen K. Painter
Debra J. Parker

Ginger Shellenberger
   Parsons
Lona D. Prasse
Kathryn M. Pumphrey
Laura Malloy Sackett
Karolyn McAdoo Shaw
Diana Upshur Smack
Carole Harding Stalling
Catherine Lynn Stovall
Page M. Sydnor
Julia Glass Waddell
Diane Matthews Walker
Jessica Bemis Ward
Ruth Drewry Wills

The following sustainer sponsors generously helped to underwrite the cost of the cookbook.

Jane Frost Bowden	Judy Frantz	Kathryn M. Pumphrey
Nancy W. Caldwell	Marie Woody Harris	Dana D. Redmond
Norvell N. Carrington	Jiggie Holt	Marlene M. Sausman
Shirley C. Caskie	Jane M. Larkin	Joan E. Swanson
Betty W. Davidson	Kathryn Cummins Mays	Emmy Lou Thomson
Constance W. Davies	Karen L. Painter	Sallie Carter Voth
Peggy Kiley Dillon	Lee Rollow Perry	Diane Matthews Walker
Dona P. Forehand	Purnell Hearn Pettyjohn	Jessica Bemis Ward

Many community members supported us by opening their homes and offering their services.

Cover Inset: Home of
  Mrs. Thomas H. Sweeney
Cover Background: Wolf Branch Farm
Introduction: Home of
  Mr. and Mrs. Lamar Cecil
First Impressions: Point of Honor
Bread and Breakfast: Home of
  Dr. and Mrs. James L. Lynde
Masterpieces: Home of
  Dr. and Mrs. Stuart H. Harris, Jr.
Finishing Touches:
  Randolph-Macon Woman's College—
  President's Home—Home of
  Mr. and Mrs. Daniel Bowman
Door to Door: Home of
  Mr. Robert L. Holloway and
  Mr. Hiram J. Gerber

City Fare: Monument Terrace—
  City of Lynchburg
Celebrations: Thomas Jefferson's Poplar Forest

James L. Blanks
Anne Radford Barrett
Mark P. Friedlander, Jr.
W. Doyle Gentry
Laura Radford Goley
Molly Roper Jenkins
Anne Martin Langley
Bill Oliver
James J. Sakalosky
Susan Schenck Stall
Judy C. Strang
Diane and Billy Walker
Our Spouses and Families

It is our sincere hope that no one has been inadvertently omitted.

In Good Company

Index

Order Information

Please send me _____ copies of *In Good Company* @ $21.95 each $ _____

Shipping and Handling @ $3.00 each $ _____

Virginia residents include sales tax @ $.99 each $ _____

Total $ _____

Name _____

Address _____

City _____ State _____ Zip _____

Daytime Phone (____) _____

Method of Payment: [   ] VISA   [   ] MasterCard

[   ] Check or Money Order payable to Junior League of Lynchburg

Account Number _____ Expiration Date _____

Signature _____

Junior League of Lynchburg, Inc.

P.O. Box 3304
Lynchburg, Virginia
24503-0304

(804) 846-6641

- -

Order Information

Please send me _____ copies of *In Good Company* @ $21.95 each $ _____

Shipping and Handling @ $3.00 each $ _____

Virginia residents include sales tax @ $.99 each $ _____

Total $ _____

Name _____

Address _____

City _____ State _____ Zip _____

Daytime Phone (____) _____

Method of Payment: [   ] VISA   [   ] MasterCard

[   ] Check or Money Order payable to Junior League of Lynchburg

Account Number _____ Expiration Date _____

Signature _____

Junior League of Lynchburg, Inc.

P.O. Box 3304
Lynchburg, Virginia
24503-0304

(804) 846-6641

Photocopies are accepted.